SoTL IN ACTION

NEW PEDAGOGIES AND PRACTICES FOR TEACHING IN HIGHER EDUCATION SERIES

Series Editor: James Rhem

Transparent Design in Higher Education Teaching and Leadership

A Guide to Implementing the Transparency Framework Institution-Wide to Improve Learning and Retention

Edited by Mary-Ann Winkelmes, Allison Boye, and Suzanne Tapp

Blended Learning

Across the Disciplines, Across the Academy

Edited by Francine S. Glazer

Clickers in the Classroom

Using Classroom Response Systems to Increase Student Learning

Edited by David S. Goldstein and Peter D. Wallis

Cooperative Learning in Higher Education

Across the Disciplines, Across the Academy

Edited by Barbara Millis

Just-in-Time Teaching

Across the Disciplines, Across the Academy

Edited by Scott Simkins and Mark Maier

Team Teaching

Across the Disciplines, Across the Academy

Edited by Kathryn M. Plank

Using Reflection and Metacognition to Improve Student Learning

Across the Disciplines, Across the Academy

Edited by Matthew Kaplan, Naomi Silver, Danielle LaVaque-Manty, and Deborah Meizlish

SoTL IN ACTION

Illuminating Critical Moments of Practice

Edited by

Nancy L. Chick

Foreword by James Rhem

STERLING, VIRGINIA

Published by Stylus Publishing, LLC.
22883 Quicksilver Drive
Sterling, Virginia 20166-2019

Library of Congress Cataloging-in-Publication Data

Names: Chick, Nancy L., 1968- editor.
Title: SoTL in action : illuminating critical moments of practice / edited by Nancy L. Chick ; foreword by James Rhem.
Description: First edition. |
Sterling, Virginia : Stylus Publishing, 2018. |
Includes index. | Includes bibliographical references.
Identifiers: LCCN 2018004268 (print) |
LCCN 2018019623 (ebook) |
ISBN 9781620366943 (Library networkable e-edition) |
ISBN 9781620366950 (Consumer e-edition) |
ISBN 9781620366929 (cloth : alk. paper) |
ISBN 9781620366936 (pbk. : alk. paper)
Subjects: LCSH: Observation (Educational method) | Effective teaching. |
Teachers--In-service training | Teachers--Professional relationships. |
Communication in education. | Education--Research--Methodology.
Classification: LCC LB1027.28 (ebook) |
LCC LB1027.28 .S66 2018 (print)
DDC 370.71/1--dc23
LC record available at https://lccn.loc.gov/2018004268

13-digit ISBN: 978-1-62036-692-9 (cloth)
13-digit ISBN: 978-1-62036-693-6 (paperback)
13-digit ISBN: 978-1-62036-694-3 (library networkable e-edition)
13-digit ISBN: 978-1-62036-695-0 (consumer e-edition)

Printed in the United States of America

All first editions printed on acid-free paper
that meets the American National Standards Institute
Z39-48 Standard.

Bulk Purchases
Quantity discounts are available for use in workshops and for staff development.
Call 1-800-232-0223

First Edition, 2018

*To Katie, Tricia, and my fellow TA Mentors
and our small, significant conversations*

CONTENTS

PART TWO: METHODS AND METHODOLOGIES

PART THREE: MAKING AN IMPACT

FOREWORD

A Brief (Somewhat) Slanted History of SoTL

In many ways the scholarship of teaching and learning (SoTL) seems new (or did a few years ago), but like most new things it has a history. Viewed from one perspective (my perspective) its history stretches back a long way and carries within it the finest values of civilization. In modern times, of course, the origins of SoTL begin with Ernest Boyer's 1990 report from the Carnegie Foundation for the Advancement of Teaching titled *Scholarship Reconsidered: Priorities of the Professoriate*. But there's longer history. Looking back to the ancient Greeks—a good place to start—Socrates saw knowledge as virtue, but whether it could be taught remained an open question. The elaborations of Plato and Aristotle didn't disagree but added, perhaps, a stronger focus on utility, an aspect American pragmatism has certainly embraced. Perhaps *virtue* is a mystery, a thread winding around and through those three great foundational ideas of civilization that fascinated the ancients—the good, the true, and the beautiful. Certainly virtue has both secular and sacred sides. Indeed, in one of the Socratic dialogues (*Meno*; Socrates, 380 BCE in Plato, 1967) virtue/knowledge seems to have a divine origin; in another (*Protagoras*; Socrates, 380 BCE in Plato, 1967) it seems quite practical.

For philosophy whether virtue/knowledge can be taught remains a mystery. In his meditation "On the Teacher," St. Augustine (389) was famously skeptical of what words do or can do, and thus skeptical of the teacher's power.

> After all who is so foolishly curious as to send his son to school to learn what the teacher thinks? When the teachers have explained by means of words all the disciplines they profess to teach, even the disciplines of virtue and of wisdom, then those who are called 'students' consider within themselves whether truths have been stated. (p. 145)

Augustine goes on to suggest that all teachers do is remind their students of what somehow they already know, an idea also found in the *Meno* and later famously echoed by Wordsworth (1807) in his "Ode: Intimations of Immortality," when he wrote "our birth is but a sleep and a forgetting" (p. 628).

While many major thinkers have given a lot of consideration to a priori ideas, they don't figure too prominently in modern thinking about teaching and learning, at least nominally. But the inquiry into how we learn and therefore how we should teach has remained insistent throughout history, and it has led to something like the insights of Socrates and Augustine. Teachers now understand that lasting learning begins in points of discovery. When all the teachers' words lead the student to an individual eureka moment, learning has occurred, and, whatever its origin, it always seems as mysterious as it is joyous. And throughout history, those called to teaching have longed to multiply these moments.

The best of those called have also acknowledged the limits of other spheres of learning to inform teaching. Early in *Talks to Teachers on Psychology*, William James (1899) cautions

> You make a great, very great mistake, if you think that psychology, being the science of the mind's laws, is something from which you can deduce definite programmes and schemes and methods of instruction for immediate schoolroom use. Psychology is a science, and teaching is an art; and sciences never generate arts directly out of themselves. (p. 145)

"Definite programmes" perhaps not, but James (1899) goes on to offer endless insights into how the mind works and therefore the best ways to provoke learning. For those called to teach, the desire to apply all we somehow know and can find out to the challenge of improving our teaching remains irresistible. The best teachers have tried to pass on insights into what they had done well and valued so highly. Renowned classics scholar Gilbert Highet's (1950) *On The Art of Teaching* stands out in my memory. Like most of the commentary on teaching that went before, it can be viewed as a kind of meditation deeply informed by both virtue (here understood as high, passionately held values) and experience.

Around the time I created The National Teaching & Learning FORUM, a book by Kenneth Eble (1994), titled *The Craft of Teaching: A Guide to Mastering the Professor's Art*, was enjoying a second edition. Also around this time, many teachers began to rankle at descriptions of teaching as an art. Calling it an art seemed to imply that some could do it and some could not, and that attitude implied a hands-off posture toward understanding and improving teaching. Hence, Eble's (1994) title tried to split the difference.

The most influential predecessor to SoTL, *Teaching Tips: Strategies, Research, and Theory for College and University Teachers* by Wilbert McKeachie (1951), had quietly followed in William James's (1899) footsteps but hadn't made provocative assertions about art or science. It offered "tips." Now in its fourteenth edition and known as *McKeachie's Teaching Tips*, it, like James, presented a blend of what psychology had found and experience had taught. As valuable as they have been, "tips" weren't enough, and the last 25 years have seen a steady stream of books looking with increasing depth into the dynamics of effective teaching. Some have been quite scientific; others more reflective. All have burnished the belief that teaching was not simply an important part of civilization, but a vital one, and that it could be improved through a deeper understanding.

For much of its social history—until quite recently actually—teaching has been regarded as the grunt-work stepchild of research. Research was seen as true scholarship, and teaching was seen as what one did to make a living. It was never true of teaching, but the prejudice had become socially powerful. That began to change with the publication of *Scholarship Reconsidered* (Boyer, 1990). Finally, it became legitimate to honor teaching as an intellectual adventure of equal value in the scholarly life as research. That shift in the discourse led to what we now know as SoTL.

SoTL has faced its challenges as it has matured in the last two decades. Was it to be all science, numbers, data? Was there a place for narrative and reflection? For the most part, contending ideas seem to have found a productive middle ground. Talk of both art and science has given way to talk of understanding and context. No one talks much of the mystery any more, but it abides. So do the faithful: they are the SoTL scholars. Can teaching be improved? We believe it can. It's the right belief to hold. After all, even the skeptical Socrates concluded "that we shall be better, braver, and more active . . . if we believe it right to look for what we do not know"(*Meno*, section 86B, 380 BCE in Plato, 1967).

James Rhem
Executive Editor
The National Teaching & Learning FORUM

References

Augustine. (389/1968). *On the teacher*. Translated by Robert P. Russell. Washington DC: Catholic University of America Press.

Boyer, E. L. (1990). *Scholarship reconsidered: Priorities of the professoriate*. Princeton, NJ: Carnegie Foundation for the Advancement of Teaching.

Eble, K. (1994). *The craft of teaching: A guide to mastering the professor's art*. San Francisco, CA: Jossey-Bass.

James, W. (1899). *Talks to teachers on psychology: And to students on some of life's ideals.* New York, NY: Henry Holt.

Highet, G. (1950). *On the art of teaching.* New York, NY: Alfred Knopf.

McKeachie, W. J. (1951/2013). *McKeachie's teaching tips: Strategies, research, and theory for college and university teachers* (14th ed.). Belmont, CA: Wadsworth Publishing.

Plato. (1967). *Plato in twelve volumes (Vol. 3).* Translated by W. R. M. Lamb. Cambridge, MA: Harvard University Press; London, England: William Heinemann Ltd.

Wordsworth, W. (1804/1919). Ode: Intimations of immortality from recollections of early childhood. In A. Quiller-Couch (Ed), *The Oxford book of English verse: 1250–1900.* Oxford, England: Oxford University Press.

INTRODUCTION

Conversations About SoTL Processes and Practices

Nancy L. Chick

When I was in graduate school in the mid-1990s, I was selected to join a group of teaching assistants from across campus to regularly come together to learn more about teaching and then to bring what we learned back to our departments. I'm sure it involved programming, structure, and specific activities, but what I remember— what lasted and what changed everything for me—were the conversations. I remember Amy in psychology talking about her research on early childhood eating patterns, and how she approached teaching the complexities of nature versus nurture. I remember Tim in biology talking about preparing and grading exams (such a different teaching experience from mine in English) and the sheer joy of his daily monitoring of . . . something . . . in his lab. I remember Pat in history talking about the tension between covering key moments in history and keeping his students interested. And I remember Tricia and Katie, our leaders, who talked about how much our teaching mattered and gave us permission to take it as seriously as our dissertations.

Twenty-something years later, it's no wonder that I'm moved by Roxå and Mårtensson's (2009) foundational research on "the conversations teachers have with colleagues" in which "teachers allow themselves to be influenced to such an extent that they develop, or even sometimes drastically change, their personal understanding of teaching and learning" (pp. 547–548). In study after study, Roxå, Mårtensson, and colleagues have established the effects of "small 'significant networks'" (Roxå & Mårtensson, 2009, p. 547) that explore teaching and learning in private, trusting, and intellectually challenging discussions. My friends and colleagues in the Teaching Assistant Mentor Program at the University of Georgia formed my first such network. Since then, conversations like these have become the soundtrack of my work life, setting the tone for everything from the kind of career I've wanted to how

I feel every time I draft a syllabus or grade an essay or walk into a classroom to how I think about students, their learning, and my role in their learning. As a scholarship of teaching and learning (SoTL) scholar, I can't overestimate the impact of these conversations.

It surprises me a little to reflect on the turn from text to conversation that led to this book. I had just finished compiling a bibliography for a SoTL primer, "a little anthology of key readings that would together provide some coverage, depth, and range of the field" (Chick, 2016). After years of trying to explain SoTL in short elevator rides, hallway conversations, e-mails, and PowerPoint slides, I dreamed of handing over a small collection of readings that would do the work for me. So I asked an unscientific sampling of friends and colleagues, "If you were putting together a SoTL primer of 1 to 10 titles to introduce colleagues to the field, what would you include?" The resulting 23 lists included 112 citations, which I distilled into 2 bibliographies: the Top 10 Citations and the Top 10 Short Pieces (see bit.ly/a-sotl-primer for the names of the contributors and these 2 lists). I'd begun looking into publishing a book of the second list when James Rhem, coeditor of the New Pedagogies and Practices in Higher Education series from Stylus Publishing, asked me to put together something like this SoTL primer but with new essays. He wanted a book on "how to do SoTL, but told primarily via examples from faculty in a spectrum of disciplines" (J. Rhem, personal communication, October 24, 2016). Rather than introducing SoTL in theory through a short collection of its key texts, this book would introduce SoTL in practice through stories of practitioners' experiences in doing SoTL.

Indeed, there are plenty of publications that define, theorize, criticize, report results of, and teach novices how to do SoTL, but there is less on doing SoTL well and seeing what it looks like. This gap reminded me of lesson study projects that aim to reveal student learning in action by "put[ting] a lesson under the microscope, to carefully analyze how students learn from our teaching and then use that knowledge to improve future performance—ours and theirs" (Cerbin, 2011, p. 2). This book is about illuminating SoTL in action by putting its critical moments under the microscope to carefully analyze how they happen and then using that knowledge to improve SoTL performance. It presents procedural vignettes that put SoTL in slow motion to help us pause, analyze, and reflect on key steps in the larger processes of doing SoTL. I thought of a series of 30-minute consultations in which a colleague wants to learn more about SoTL and get started on his or her first project. This framework invokes that power of informal, intellectually challenging conversations with trusted colleagues (Roxå & Mårtensson, 2009). I recruited people I'd actually had (or overheard) conversations with about these critical moments, and I encouraged them to use the voices and approaches they'd use in a consultation. The result is that the chapters draw from different sources—some are grounded in the existing literature, many in the contributors' own experiences, and a few in hypothetical situations or even in metaphor.

The chapters in Part One discuss the strong foundations of SoTL projects. Gary Poole talks about the authentic origins of SoTL projects, those moments of curiosity in which we confront our beliefs about teaching and learning that are grounded in intuition, anecdote, and observation. Anthony Ciccone follows with "the ultimate SoTL moment . . . when a relatively common teaching problem, on reflection, opens a broad panorama of interesting and challenging questions about learners and learning" (p. 17, this volume). Margy MacMillan discusses one of the necessary responses to our questions, the elusive SoTL literature review, which is "a process and a product" (p. 23, this volume) that grounds a project in prior work and assumptions strong enough for "bearing the weight of practice" (p. 25, this volume). As a literature review brings up the relationship between SoTL and educational research, Kimberley A. Grant pushes back against knee-jerk characterizations of contrast and conflict and instead talks about the common ground of the broader field of teaching and learning. Acknowledging that SoTL is situated in this broader field, as well as across our own disciplines, Carol Berenson encourages us to articulate the tradition of inquiry and its assumptions that undergird our specific approaches to research. Robin Mueller follows with how she thinks about another critical moment in conceptualizing a SoTL project, namely, aligning its research methods with its purpose. Ryan C. Martin tackles the contentious and misunderstood requirement of seeking an ethics review, necessary for SoTL as research involving human participants but also, he argues, as part of SoTL's overarching purpose of doing good.

In Part Two, the contributors put SoTL in slow motion, explaining what it looks like to carry out specific methods that make student learning visible. Trent W. Maurer cautions us in our selection of survey methods and looks to the frequent choice of questionnaires with plenty of advice on how to use them well. Bill Cerbin shares his process for conducting classroom observations to bring him closer to understanding what's actually happening as students are learning or having difficulty with learning. Janice Miller-Young talks about interviewing students to "see what is otherwise unobservable" and collecting "compelling stories that challenge our assumptions about the realities and experiences of our students" (p. 98, this volume). Karen Manarin describes how she slows down and closely reads student artifacts, a process similar to "a case study that if done well suggests something about other texts or contexts" (p. 101, this volume). Similarly, Lendol Calder shows how think-alouds have allowed him to "eavesdro[p] on students while they made sense of historical materials" (p. 115, this volume), giving him insights into otherwise inaccessible moments in their learning.

In Part Three, the contributors encourage us to think about the sites where SoTL has the potential to make an impact beyond our own practice. Jessie L. Moore talks us through some steps of describing a SoTL project in writing to "pu[t] our work in conversation with prior scholarship and ope[n] up portals for others to respond to our research, add to it, and continue the dialogue for years to come" (p. 125, this volume). To help encourage written SoTL, David J. Voelker shares his thoughts on how and why to read these publications, which may require "translation as we convert insights and meanings from one discipline or context into another" (p. 127, this volume), that keep us reflecting on and potentially revising our practice. In thinking about how SoTL made public can ultimately have local impacts, Dan Bernstein recalls his experiences with course portfolios and other "practical" and "publicly accessible learning objects" that are "incredibly powerful as change agents in the culture of higher education practice" (p. 142, this volume). Jennifer Meta Robinson describes her ideal SoTL conference and how it compares to the "composite afterimage of the many academic conferences [she has] attended" (p. 143, this volume).

Ultimately, this book isn't strictly about how to do SoTL. Instead, it's a book about how 16 scholars do SoTL. Each chapter presents the experience, advice, and voice of a single scholar, but as Manarin and Voelker remind us about reading the works of others, each chapter also suggests something about other contexts, inviting us to translate the writer's insights into our own. In the end, the chapters also reflect what we've learned from SoTL itself about student learning: the importance of questioning what we intuit, exploring and articulating the sources of those intuitions and assumptions, aligning our practices with our intentions, planning to do good, making visible what we've taken for granted, and purposefully thinking through the effects and impacts of our work.

References

Cerbin, B. (2011). *Lesson study: Using classroom inquiry to improve teaching and learning in higher education.* Sterling, VA: Stylus.

Chick, N. (2016, Sept. 21). A SoTL primer. [Web log post]. Retrieved from http://sotl.ucalgaryblogs.ca/2016/09/21/a-sotl-primer/

Roxå, T., & Mårtensson, K. (2009). Significant conversations and significant networks: Exploring the backstage of the teaching arena. *Studies in Higher Education, 34,* 547–559. doi:10.1080/03075070802597200

PART ONE

STRONG FOUNDATIONS

I

USING INTUITION, ANECDOTE, AND OBSERVATION

Rich Sources of SoTL Projects

Gary Poole

W hat if inside every teacher was a scholarship of teaching and learning (SoTL) project waiting to be brought to life? I believe this is a real possibility because the act of teaching is so cerebral, so academic, and so social that it is impossible to engage in it without developing an internal system of beliefs about what is or isn't going on. In this chapter, I take a closer look at how these beliefs can become curiosities and how these in turn become the origins of SoTL projects. In doing so, we need to explore some of the sources of our beliefs about teaching and learning. I look at three main sources: our intuitions, our anecdotal experiences, and our direct observations.

Intuition, anecdotes, and observation live close to home for us in our thinking, our interactions with others, and our direct experience. This personal relevance yields a rich collection of beliefs that can pertain to anything and everything related to teaching and learning, from how people learn to what constitutes effective teaching in a particular context. At the same time, these beliefs can vary considerably in their veracity. It is this compelling combination of important richness and varying accuracy that makes for great starting points for SoTL work.

One way to think about this is to problematize our thinking, using the word *problem* as Bass (1999) uses it. Problems are not negative things; rather, they are interesting challenges for the scientist and humanist within us.

Regehr (2010) presented a clear contrast between research intended to solve something as opposed to research intended to explore something.

Although this might help us understand the source of many SoTL projects, we should not fall into the trap of believing that all SoTL projects must solve a problem. Some will provide elegantly insightful descriptions of a learning process or environment.

From Beliefs to Curiosities

For our rich beliefs to become motivators of SoTL projects, they must first be transformed into curiosities. This happens using general questions such as, Is this belief about teaching and learning really true? or What are the implications of this belief? It is when we become curious about our beliefs that we are motivated to examine them through research. Thus, sources of our beliefs, such as intuition, anecdote, and observation, can become sources of our curiosity, which in turn become the origins of SoTL projects. This process is presented in Figure 1.1.

Because they are fundamental to an understanding of the ways many SoTL projects find life, our exploration is organized around the three starting elements in the flow chart: intuition, anecdote, and observation.

Intuition as a Source of SoTL Project Ideas

Intuition (n.d.) is defined as "any quick insight, recognized immediately without a reasoning process." Similarly, Benner and Tanner (1987) define *intuition* as "judgment without rationale" (p. 23). These definitions are consistent with Daniel Kahneman's (2011) notion of System 1 thinking.

According to Kahneman (2011), much of our thinking takes place at a rapid pace, relying on assumptions and intuitions that are quickly accessed from memory. He contrasts this high-speed System 1 thinking with System 2 thinking, which is much more plodding and deliberate. When we engage in System 2 thinking, we take the time to question those assumptions and intuitions. We collect more information, and we reflect more on it. In essence, SoTL projects that find their origin in our intuition represent our

Figure 1.1. How SoTL projects flow from intuition, anecdote, and observation.

way of moving from System 1 to System 2 thinking about our teaching and students' learning.

It isn't easy to reflect on intuition, however. We must expose what is often unexamined and automatic. Marano (2004) underscores the inherent paradox in this process when she observes, "The act of

Kahneman (2011) helps us see how SoTL projects may find their origin in our intuition but then move from fast thinking to slow deliberate thinking about our teaching and our students' learning.

reflecting on intuition is precisely what intuition isn't" (para. 5). Furthermore, intuition can yield such deeply engrained beliefs that we simply aren't curious about these beliefs; rather, we see them as self-evident truths. Thus, there hardly seems to be any point in mounting a SoTL project to test what is intuitive.

But it is exactly this way of thinking—that intuition is self-evident—that makes it a vital and necessary source of SoTL projects. In teaching and learning, we must systematically examine what we take to be obvious because it so often turns out to be anything but. See Table 1.1 for some examples of beliefs we might hold intuitively, and for which research might tell a different story.

TABLE 1.1
Some Intuitive Beliefs That Might Not Be Supported by Research

The Belief	*The Research*
Today's students prefer to learn in groups or teams.	Students might not prefer group work because they sometimes feel they are expected to deal with complex social dynamics in group work without much support from instructors (Hillyard, Gillespie, & Littig, 2010).
Today's students are skilled multitaskers because they are frequently juggling information from a range of devices and sources.	In a study of American and European students, the tendency to multitask was negatively associated with academic performance. The effect was most pronounced in the American sample (Karpinski et al., 2013).
Learning styles are tantamount to stable traits that do not change over time.	Although some approaches to learning carry over from one situation to the next, it would be more accurate to think of learning styles as approaches to a learning task that are, at the very least, dependent on the nature of the task (Cassidy, 2010; Loo, 1997). They are not the same as personality traits.

There is a large amount of literature on the fallibility of intuition (Chabris & Simons, 2010). Yet it would be a serious mistake to dismiss intuition out of hand, especially when it comes from experienced practitioners. Indeed, effective System 1 thinking is a defining characteristic of expertise. At the same time, it is also a source of things like medical error (Croskerry, 2009). Again, these two possibilities—intuition as fallible yet also the stuff of expert thinking—make intuition so fascinating and important as a source of SoTL project work.

For example, our intuitions about how people learn may well be born from an understanding of how we learn. If we believe our learning flourishes in collaborative settings, then we might conclude that all people learn best by collaboration. There will be times when this intuition is correct and others when it is not, and this is where a SoTL project waits to be brought to life.

Anecdotes and the Power of Conversations

Roxå and Mårtensson's (2009) work illuminates why anecdotal data are so powerful: Our conversations, which are often rich in narrative, are particularly memorable.

We are beginning to develop a better understanding of how informal conversations with colleagues affect our understanding of teaching and learning.

Roxå and Mårtensson's (2009) identification of what they call "small significant networks" (p. 547) indicates that our beliefs about teaching and learning are shaped in part when we express ideas to others and they express their ideas to us. Our conversations within these networks are an important source of anecdotal data because these conversations are often rich in narrative, making them particularly memorable compared to, for example, a paper we read. When a colleague says, "You won't believe what happened in my second-year class today," we are hooked.

It has been suggested that we select our network members astutely with a preference for those we believe share similar views and may have had similar experiences (Poole, Verwoord, & Iqbal, 2017). Although this selection strategy might be comforting and reaffirming, it runs the risk of ensuring that we confirm rather than examine our views about teaching and learning and that we do so with what appears to be trusted data that are rarely questioned. However, just as intuition may vary between being fallible and insightful, so too can the anecdotes we share in our conversations in networks. Anecdotal evidence, just like intuition, becomes an excellent source of ideas for SoTL projects. This requires us to hear the conversational contributions of colleagues not as statements of truth but as hypotheses.

We've all had conversations with a colleague who talks about "students these days." (See Poole et al. [2017] for a description of ways we might talk about this.) How did that conversation go? Did it start with, "I have some hypotheses about student motivation based on my experiences in the classroom. It would be good to test those"? Or did it start more simply with, "Students these days are so entitled and consumer-oriented that they can be very hard to teach"? If we start with the latter statement, the conversation is more likely to provide opportunities to vent one's emotions than originate a SoTL project. Significant networks are good venues for venting, and such venting might at times be a healthy thing to do. However, it rarely moves us forward in our pursuit of excellence in teaching and learning. As suggested in the first statement, there may be reasons to suspect that some students exhibit a high sense of entitlement. Testing this is warranted and necessary and would make a very good SoTL project. We need to turn our beliefs about students into curiosities because these beliefs, especially when based on emotionally charged conversations with others, might be less than accurate.

Of course we know that anecdotes are not truths in themselves. They do, however, have the power of truth, referred to as *narrative truth* (Spence, 1982). A good story told well is not just attention-getting and memorable. It usually feels true. This is especially the case if it is told by a trusted colleague. As Weinbaum (1999) states in her juxtaposition of narrative truth and fact, we may well "forge a truth that is better held together by the force of narrative rhetoric and metaphor than by fact" (p. 1). This is one reason anecdotal evidence is a valuable place to begin a SoTL project—in this case about the characteristics of students in a particular context.

Observation: What You See Is What You Question

Just as becoming curious about our gut-level or anecdotal beliefs about teaching and learning (rather than simply accepting them) motivates us to take those SoTL projects from within us and bring them to life, so too do our curiosities about what we observe. It would seem, though, that the things we observe firsthand are least likely to be subject to bias and, therefore, do not need to be tested by a SoTL project. For example, we see with our own eyes that those students who choose to sit at the back of a lecture hall are less engaged than students who sit toward the front. As another example, we encounter students who come to our office to complain about a grade on an assignment, and that complaint seems to lack substance. These things happen, and we see them clearly.

However, with every observation there are at least three important questions we should ask. First, How prevalent is this thing that I have just observed? Second, If it really has happened frequently, how should I best respond? And third, Is there something about me that causes me to observe things this way when others would not? In other words, does this observation illuminate more about me or the situation being observed? How might this observation have been filtered through my own particular assumptions and visions of the world? This final question might be a bit more difficult to answer. It calls for a kind of SoTL project featuring considerable introspection and reflection requiring a level of objectivity that can be hard to summon on one's own. Still, it can yield excellent and publishable work.

Ascertaining the real frequency of a phenomenon requires more systematic observation than we normally have the time or inclination for in our day-to-day lives. Given such constraints, we suppress our curiosity about the belief. Those students sitting at the back of the room who appear disengaged don't tend to be the ones we approach before or after class, even for an informal conversation to get a sense of their engagement. In contrast, imagine a project in which we used measures of engagement and mapped students' engagement scores according to where they sat in the room. If we were to do this for a number of classes, we would develop some measure of how frequently disengaged students sit in the back. We might also conduct interviews with students to gain further insights. Through this research, we might find that the initial observation was upheld, but then again maybe not. Similarly, it would also be a good idea for us to actually count the number of times students complain about grading either in person or in e-mail, as well as the number of times those complaints came without substance. There are psychological reasons we might overestimate the frequency of such occurrences. Such incidents are unpleasant, and we have a tendency to overestimate the frequency of unpleasant incidents because they are recalled relatively easily (Hertel, Maydon, Cottle, & Vrijsen, 2017). This effect is heightened if we ruminate on such incidents, as we sometimes do.

If a SoTL project reveals that the observed phenomenon does occur as frequently as we thought, then what is to be done? If students are complaining about grades without providing any rationale, could this be addressed early in the course? We might say something like,

> I am happy to talk to you about why you received the grade you did. That is how we learn. If you are going to initiate this conversation, please come with an explanation of why you are not clear on the rationale for your grade.

Perhaps students could write out these explanations. SoTL projects can be designed to determine the extent to which these strategies affect discussions about grades, not to mention developing a better understanding of students' motives for particular grade concerns. They are not all motivated by a simple desire for a higher grade.

In sum, SoTL projects can originate from the things we feel, hear, and see related to teaching and learning. For such projects to come to life, we must become curious, reflect on all this, design good questions based on those reflections, and then craft appropriate methods to help us answer those questions. These processes are discussed throughout this book.

A Final Word: Researching Things That Matter to Us Personally

SoTL projects that originate in our intuitions, anecdotes, and observations often feature a high degree of personal investment. On the one hand, we might predict that beliefs we care deeply about will be the ones we are most motivated to explore. Our greatest curiosities lie in these beliefs. On the other hand, there is an inherent risk in developing curiosities regarding our strongly held beliefs. The results of a SoTL project may or may not support those beliefs. The lively and very enjoyable exercise we've been doing in class for the past four years that students seem to like so much may prove to actually have little effect on student learning or retention.

This is the way it is when we have the courage to attempt a systematic investigation of those deeply held intuitions about how learning works and what students are like. This also applies to the anecdotal examples we hear from trusted and well-liked colleagues. We might have good reason to believe that a SoTL project stemming from those anecdotes would support them; however, there is also a chance that we just can't get the data to support what that anecdote seems to be screaming at us so loudly and clearly. It can be disquieting to challenge or even change our beliefs about what people are like. We think we know their attributes and motives. If we don't know these things, we might feel helpless, or at least socially clueless. This helps explain why it isn't easy to accept data that contradict what we think we know about our students and how they learn.

Perhaps most vexing of all is a SoTL project that sets out to test the veracity of the things we have encountered with our own eyes and ears. Research of any kind can get somewhat maddening when, for one reason or another, we can't seem to replicate what we have observed. Is it possible that our observation was a one-off occurrence? Is it possible that, in fact, our observations were filtered through our views of how the world works, and so those observations were less than accurate? Were those students as enamored with that classroom exercise as we thought they were? Is it possible their facial expressions and postures during class were misleading, or our confidence in understanding student preferences is a bit misplaced? Not a comforting thought.

Here, then, is the inherent risk in pursuing the SoTL project that lies waiting within us. Good research in any field is not guaranteed to confirm our views of the world. If it is just confirmation we want, we can find a like-minded colleague or friend who will provide that for us. If, however, we want to truly improve teaching and learning, we must breathe life into those SoTL projects that lie within us.

References

Bass, R. (1999). The scholarship of teaching: What's the problem? *Inventio, 1*(1), 1–9.

Benner, P., & Tanner, C. (1987). Clinical judgment: How expert nurses use intuition. *American Journal of Nursing, 87,* 23–31.

Cassidy, S. (2010). Learning styles: An overview of theories, models, and measures. *Educational Psychology, 24,* 419–444.

Chabris, C., & Simons, D. (2010). *The invisible gorilla: And other ways our intuitions deceive us.* New York, NY: Crown.

Croskerry, P. (2009). Clinical cognition and diagnostic error: Applications of a dual process model of reasoning. *Advances in Health Science Education, 14,* 27–35.

Hertel, P. T., Maydon, A., Cottle, J., & Vrijsen, J. N. (2017). Cognitive bias modification: Retrieval practice to simulate and oppose ruminative memory biases. *Clinical Psychological Science, 5,* 122–130.

Hillyard, C., Gillespie, D., & Littig, P. (2010). University students' attitudes about learning in small groups after frequent participation. *Active Learning in Higher Education, 11*(1), 9–20.

Intuition. (n.d.). In *Merriam-Webster's Online Dictionary* (11th ed.). Retrieved from https://www.merriam-webster.com/dictionary/intuition

Kahneman, D. (2011). *Thinking fast and slow.* New York, NY: Farrar, Strauss and Giroux.

Karpinski, A. C., Kirschner, P. A., Ozer, I., Mellott, J. A., & Ochwo, P. (2013). An exploration of social networking site use, multitasking, and academic performance among United States and European university students. *Computers in Human Behavior. 29,* 1182–1192.

Loo, R. (1997). Evaluating change and stability in learning style scores: A methodological concern. *Educational Psychology, 17,* 95–100.

Marano, H. E. (2004, May 4). Trusting intuition: Sometimes we think too much, then become paralyzed in the process. *Psychology Today.* Retrieved from https://www.psychologytoday.com/articles/200405/trusting-intuition-0

Poole, G., Verwoord, R., & Iqbal, I. (2017). Small significant networks as birds of a feather. Manuscript submitted for publication.

Regehr, G. (2010). It's not rocket science: Rethinking our metaphors for research in health professions education. *Medical Education, 44,* 31–39.

Roxå, T. & Mårtensson, K. (2009). Significant conversations and significant networks: Exploring the backstage of the teaching arena. *Studies in Higher Education, 34,* 547–559.

Spence, D. P. (1982). *Narrative truth and historical truth: Meaning and interpretation in psychoanalysis.* New York, NY: Norton.

Weinbaum, B. (1999). Narrative vs historical truth: Insights from field work in right-wing popular consciousness in Israel. *Women in Judaism, 2*(1), 1–16.

2

LEARNING MATTERS

Asking Meaningful Questions

Anthony Ciccone

Success *is defined by students not only as learning lots about a subject, but knowing how they learned it and why what they learned matters to their understanding and interaction with the world around them. (Kreber, 2009, p. 4)*

If you ask a question, the machine begins to feel less like a machine. (Gawande, 2007, p. 252)

Readers of this book likely have an ongoing passion for teaching and learning. They examine and update their own courses regularly, work closely with colleagues with similar interests, and may even contribute their expertise to department and campus-wide initiatives. Scholarly inquiry into the effect of their work on understanding and improving student learning seems like a natural next step. I hope this chapter will encourage that passion by offering a process for formulating and pursuing meaningful scholarship of teaching and learning (SoTL) questions.

Those of us engaged in SoTL work have noticed that our questions often emerge from the very personal experience of encountering a problem in our teaching and learning context. This troubling experience piques our natural curiosity as professionals to reflect on complex situations, to ponder ways to understand them better, and to imagine different ways to approach the issues involved. The process of noticing, reflecting, and imagining problematizes the experience (Bass, 1999), thus making the place where teaching and learning intersect a true object of scholarly inquiry and not just something to guess at or tinker with. Our teaching and learning "problems" become research "opportunities" as our curiosity transforms perplexity into interesting, consequential questions (Huber & Hutchings, 2005).

If SoTL is at its core systematic inquiry into teaching and learning made public, its value and success depend on the questions we ask about these perplexing teaching and learning experiences; more specifically, SoTL asks us to frame questions that are meaningful for ourselves; our students; our colleagues; and, ultimately, for advancing the field. Formulating and pursuing challenging SoTL questions enables us to join an ongoing conversation about understanding and enhancing student learning and our role in furthering it.

From my experience in teaching and researching a freshman seminar on comedy and my years helping colleagues pursue their own SoTL projects, I have found that meaningful SoTL inquiry can arise when our questions meet five conditions.

The first condition is that our question should arise from a troubling, surprising, or perplexing teaching and learning experience that seems to defy a simple solution. We can all recall moments when something a student said or wrote raised surprising issues. As good teachers, we put ourselves on the alert for these moments, for example, an exam question no one seems to understand, a writing assignment that evokes two completely different sets of responses, a class discussion that reveals serious misunderstandings of a concept or a skill, or a student response that forces us to reflect on how and why we go about our work and what we're actually accomplishing. For me, a moment like that came in my freshman seminar on comedy.

Huber and Hutchings (2005) provide extensive examples of SoTL questions from a variety of fields and interesting examples of the inquiry process.

We were doing some work in pairs, brainstorming ideas about what made a certain skit funny. There was the usual discussion on topic, then fewer and fewer pairs on task. As I stood to the side and observed, I probably sighed or made some other audible sign of exasperation. At that moment, Tom—the always observant class smart aleck—must have picked up on it and asked me out of the blue, "How do you go on, Ciccone?" Taken aback, I mumbled my usual, "Well, after 30 years, you get used to it. I'll get it right next time. Things will get better," and then I turned to his partner, Dan, and asked him what he thought I should do. "I don't know," Dan replied. "All I know is I wouldn't want to have to teach me."

I had chosen comedy as the course subject and formulating one's own theory of how it worked as the course learning goal because I believed that students learn better when they are deeply and personally engaged with a topic and task. Working in pairs was an essential part of my teaching toward this goal. From this perspective, Tom's and Dan's remarks were particularly troubling and surprising. Having noticed a problem, or more precisely, having had the problem brought to my attention, how could I respond?

The second condition for a good SoTL question is met when we arrive at something truly consequential to us as teachers and to our students as learners. The failure of my think-pair-share activity invited a certain type of instrumental or "what works?" question (Hutchings, 2000, p. 4): How could I do this better? Typically, I might have reviewed the literature on facilitating small-group interaction, implemented a new strategy to see if it increased engagement in the task in contrast to the earlier attempt, and asked students for their opinions. But is this type of question, the first type of SoTL inquiry, really what the situation called for?

If I took this approach, I'd address only the most visible part of the problem, the lack of engagement with the task, without really knowing what else lay below the surface. My failed pair activity seemed to have opened more profound and consequential lines of inquiry. Dan's remark, "I wouldn't want to have to teach me," reminded me that I really knew very little about how students understand (and think about) what they are doing in my course. As a humanist, this especially touched a nerve. Where does a remark like that come from? How can I get at what it means? In my desire to deploy engaging teaching activities, had I missed the learner part of the equation? How could I know what, if any, effect I was having on how students saw themselves as learners?

Tom's question ("How do you go on, Ciccone?") was equally troubling. Where did I see the value in the struggle? Why did I believe this course was worth it to my students? Did my course really make clear to my students the habits of mind or dispositions toward learning I felt were worth acquiring? Did they share my vision? These questions certainly raised consequential lines of inquiry. In my experience, the ultimate SoTL moment occurs, as in this case, when a relatively common teaching problem, on reflection, opens a broad panorama of interesting and challenging questions about learners and learning. My professional development workshops became true SoTL programs when participants made this shift as well.

The third condition for a good SoTL question is met when we find ourselves required to gather new and different information about our students' learning or at least look differently at what we've been getting and thus to teach and assess differently.

Hutchings's (2005) seminal taxonomy of questions contains examples of foundational work by Carnegie scholars. See especially Cerbin's chapter 9, in this book.

Once we move past the What would work better? approach, we reach what Hutchings (2000) has called a second type of SoTL inquiry, the What is happening here? question. My troubling experience invited me to ask, very broadly, What's going on in my students' minds when they approach the course topics? or perhaps, How do my students understand what they're doing? Could I focus these questions on my essential course goals and find out something important and useful about how well the students were achieving them?

Dan's remark reminded me of my goal to help students think with and for complexity, and thus to become more comfortable with the ongoing ambiguity that type of thinking creates. Did I have any indication that students were making progress on these two specific goals? What might that progress look like? These questions seemed more manageable, but they would require changes in approach to advance the goals and to gather information about that progress. Were there others who eschewed the need to think with greater complexity and enjoyed, as one student put it, analyzing the comedies while remaining disappointed that I had never revealed the definitive theory of comedy?

This is another typical moment in the development of a SoTL inquiry. After formulating an interesting question about how well students are accomplishing broad learning goals, we ask where students have the chance to perform those goals and thus produce evidence we can study. The information we can glean for studying learning goals that really matter—experiencing and valuing diversity, reaching deep understanding, thinking in a disciplinary or interdisciplinary way, thinking with and for complexity—is usually sparse and indirect at best. We thus design new activities and assignments that will produce more direct, visible evidence of the students' thinking and learning. This shift requires us to teach and assess differently, making SoTL inquiry fundamentally communicative. That is, it begins and evolves responsively with the evidence of student learning (Bernstein & Bass, 2005). As the inquiry and early results deepen our understanding, meaningful SoTL questions challenge us to adjust our pedagogical strategies to respond to what we're learning about our students' learning.

Fortunately, SoTL researchers often find they have already begun to collect useful information without really knowing it. My precourse assignment asked students to provide their first ideas about comedy, humor, and laughter. Their responses indicated that when it came to understanding complex phenomena, many seemed naturally inclined to a type of spontaneous, unreflective interpretation of experience. They want to believe that things are as they appear, so their first understanding is sufficient: Something is either funny or it's not; funny is what we laugh at and vice versa. Put another way, we might ask, Why do people laugh? Seems like a simple question. It's a natural reaction. If my goal was to move them from the natural reaction explanation into complexity and to accepting or indeed valuing the

ambiguity raised by complex thinking, these responses to my precourse
assignment not only defined my
teaching challenge (its original purpose) but also served as a baseline for
describing initial thinking and measuring future progress.

*Ciccone, Meyers, & Waldemann
(2008) trace the earlier stages of the
SoTL inquiry referred to in this chapter and provide more information on
the student learning we uncovered.*

The only way I could learn if
my students were beginning to
think differently was to ask them directly through a kind of periodic, reflective think-aloud. I introduced opportunities for students to reflect on their
learning, to think about not only what they were learning (content and
skills) but also how their thinking about the course topics was changing.
After 10 weeks, I asked them to reflect on what they'd learned so far about
comedy, laughter, and humor; how their thinking might have changed; and
what questions had become (or remained) important to them. As starting
points, they used what they had written for the precourse assignment and
an earlier summary of what they found interesting and challenging from the
first class. Note the connection between pedagogy and inquiry here: The
reflective assignments encouraged new ways of thinking as they provided
evidence of the same. My SoTL questions evolved as well: Were students
making progress toward thinking with and for complexity on the course
topics? How could I describe this progress? Relying on our own close reading of student responses for patterns and themes, and the work of John
Dewey (1934), 2 colleagues (experts in qualitative analysis not involved
with the course) and I were able to discern an interesting set of categories
that described how the students moved closer to thinking with and for complexity about comedy (Ciccone, Meyers, & Waldmann, 2008)

But this analysis could not account for all the reflections we received,
which brings us to the fourth condition for a good SoTL research question:
Our question should raise more questions than it answers and thus invite
further research.

If Dan's and Tom's remarks were surprising, two student responses to
How has your thinking about comedy and laughter changed? also stopped
me in my tracks. One student wrote, "I have learned that you can never
discuss, analyze, listen, comprehend, and reflect enough to really understand the meaning of something," generalizing the complexity of learning
and its processes. The second student wrote, "I don't accept things as just
simple ideas anymore. I engage myself to reflect more now and not just
accept what is given to me as right and wrong," revealing how thinking with complexity about comedy affected behavior and values. These

responses hinted at what Timmermans (2010) and others have called "epistemological and ontological changes" (p. 3); that is, changes in how we understand how knowledge is acquired and how that knowledge can change who we are.

Thus, after the What is? and What works? questions, a third type of SoTL question emerges: What would happen if we asked about these effects? (Hutchings, 2000). Again, I needed more direct information, so I added the following to the 10-week reflection: Based on your experiences in this class, how has your thinking changed about what learning is and what it is for? In addition, to find out if students came to a deeper understanding of themselves while learning to think with and for complexity, I redesigned the final paper guidelines to include the evolution and the results of their newly found understanding. These reflections produced a wealth of evidence about how students experienced their confrontation with complexity and ambiguity as they moved through the course topics.

The fifth condition for a good SoTL research question is fulfilled when, as in this case, our question shows the potential to go beyond the problem from whence it arose to elucidate some key insights into the big issues about student learning and the frameworks that would explain them.

SoTL inquiry may arise from classroom issues, but these issues are often part of larger investigations into learning that various frameworks have tried to account for. In my case, a colleague suggested that my results might have implications for the threshold concepts framework (Meyer & Land, 2003), which suggests there are essential concepts, habits of mind, or dispositions that if not understood or mastered block progress in learning the discipline. It describes the stages students may pass through when confronting this "new and previously inaccessible way of thinking about something" and acquiring a "transformed way of understanding, or interpreting, or viewing something" (Meyer & Land, 2003, p. 1) that unblocks progress.

This framework did indeed help us describe how students confront, struggle with, and ultimately pass through the essential and troubling confrontation with complexity and ambiguity. As such, it complemented our earlier taxonomy by filling in the liminal spaces (Meyer & Land, 2003) between the stages of thinking students acquired. But in using it to understand the evolution of thinking with and for complexity, we uncovered a possible extension of the framework. Threshold concepts were not just related to the acquisition of content or skills that transformed what one came to know about a subject, there were also threshold concepts such as this one that when acquired had the potential to transform the self as a learner (epistemologically) and as an actor in the world (ontologically).

SoTL studies teaching in the context of its effects on student learning. We're usually not looking for a better way to use small-group learning, for example, but rather what we can find out about student learning through its use—a subtle but essential difference. Once we've made learning the center of our inquiry, we can think about it as a product and a process. Although inquiry into content acquired and skills developed may be interesting and even essential, significant contributions remain to be made through inquiry into the process in which students experience changes in their ways of thinking and being through our courses (see Figure 2.1).

In the reflections on their own passages through thinking about comedy with and for complexity, students provided ample indications that they were changing in these ways. As one student put it,

> As we begin to think more critically we come to ask ourselves "Why does any of this matter?" Or, "What value does humor possess?" As my views of laughter and humor have developed, I have come to believe they are fundamental to the human condition. Humor allows us to deal with life, and stress, and social scenarios that we are otherwise unprepared for. . . . Humor allows us to just step back for a moment, and think and analyze.

I offer this path toward asking meaningful questions to encourage us to think of SoTL inquiry not merely as a way to examine the effectiveness of certain teaching strategies but more importantly as a way to learn more about the broader skills our students acquire and even, perhaps, about the changes in how they understand and value learning. SoTL inquiry can help

Figure 2.1. A learning taxonomy.

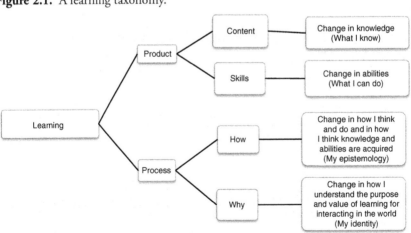

us move beyond the classroom problem at hand to engage colleagues from other disciplines with similar interests in, as showcased here, the value of student reflection, how students experience our courses and how they deal with complexity and ambiguity. We're quite far from studying another small-group strategy that improves engagement and perhaps closer to understanding how and why we and our students go on.

References

Bass, R. (1999). The scholarship of teaching: What's the problem? *Inventio, 1*(1), 1–10.

Bernstein, D., & Bass, R. (2005). The scholarship of teaching and learning. *Academe, 91*(4), 37–43.

Ciccone, A., Meyers, R. A., & Waldmann, S. (2008). What's so funny? Moving students toward complex thinking in a course on comedy and laughter. *Arts and Humanities in Higher Education, 7*(3), 308–322.

Dewey, J. (1934) *How we think: A restatement of the relation of reflective thinking to the educative process.* Chicago, IL: D. C. Heath.

Gawande, A. (2007). *Better: A surgeon's notes on performance.* New York, NY: Henry Holt.

Huber, M., & Hutchings, P. (2005). *The advancement of learning: Building the teaching commons.* San Francisco, CA: Jossey-Bass.

Hutchings, P. (2000). *Opening lines: Approaches to the scholarship of teaching and learning.* Menlo Park, CA: Carnegie Foundation for the Advancement of Teaching.

Kreber, C. (2009). *The university and its disciplines.* New York, NY: Routledge.

Meyer, J., & Land, R. (2003). *Threshold concepts and troublesome knowledge: Linkages to ways of thinking and practicing within the disciplines.* Retrieved from http://www.etl.tla.ed.ac.uk/docs/ETLreport4.pdf

Timmermans, J. A. (2010). Changing our minds: The developmental potential of threshold concepts. In J. H. F. Meyer, R. Land, & C. Baillie (Eds.), *Threshold concepts and transformational learning* (pp. 3–19). Rotterdam, The Netherlands: Sense.

3

THE SoTL
LITERATURE REVIEW

Exploring New Territory

Margy MacMillan

I n this chapter, I look at the scholarship of teaching and learning (SoTL) literature review as a process and a product, as these are intertwined. Reviewing the literature is an iterative process that occurs throughout a study, identifying patterns, gaps, key voices, and missing perceptions. Writing the literature review as product synthesizes prior work, draws together theory and practice, uses foundational ideas to illuminate current research, and sets the stage for the study. It also requires an understanding of readers and of the authors' responsibilities to the discipline. That's a tall order for any task, and it is especially challenging in SoTL, given the nature of the literature in the field. Unfortunately, the literature review often suffers from a sort of benign neglect, as researchers (understandably) tend to find the processes of conducting their own study, gathering their own data, and sharing their own results more exciting than synthesizing the work of others. Reconceptualizing the literature as data and synthesis of the literature as a meaningful result of the study in and of itself is the first step to getting more out of the literature review process as a researcher, as well as providing a product that benefits readers and SoTL as a discipline.

The Necessity of the SoTL Literature Review

For researchers, immersion in the literature is critical from the very beginning of a project. The SoTL literature review not only strengthens the final product of a project but also benefits the entire process. Understanding the relevant theory and prior work can help researchers design studies that align more closely with their questions. For instance, reading how other scholars have perceived the underlying barriers affecting learners in a particular situation may lead to a more focused understanding and therefore to a more focused, more easily researchable question. Delving into educational theory also helps articulate the researcher's own conceptions of teaching and learning, useful in examining the assumptions that might reduce the quality of a study (Miller-Young & Yeo, 2015). The work of others can save researchers time by providing examples of qualitative or quantitative instruments and protocols, criteria for analyzing results, and models for writing. These are particularly useful in SoTL where projects may draw from a range of research traditions and where there are fewer default road maps for investigations. As Hutchings, Huber, and Ciccone (2011) note, "The writing process not only focuses one's attention on one's own work but has a marvelous way of lighting up the work of others, bringing what might otherwise go unnoticed into one's sphere of interest and analysis" (pp. 37–38). Savory, Burnett, and Goodburn (2007) similarly see prior work as a generative starting point in their excellent guide to contextualizing SoTL work in the field. They note aspects to watch for, such as context and the measurement of variables that can lead to a clearer understanding of how a new project might be different or to a change in the researcher's plans.

For readers, the literature sets the stage for the work. Just as the literature of SoTL spans the disciplines, so does its audience, which adds an extra authorial responsibility. In discipline-specific writing, researchers may assume that readers have a working knowledge of more or less the same literature as they do, but the same assumptions cannot be made in SoTL. In fact, it is reasonable to proceed as though a paper were the very first SoTL work a reader has encountered. Interest in SoTL is growing rapidly, and readers often come into the field with very little advance preparation. Also, not everyone who reads and uses the SoTL literature is a researcher, which again may impose a responsibility on the literature review that may not be present in other contexts. Considering what a reader will need to know to understand the manuscript and use it in teaching or research will inform what should be included in the literature review. In a field where the research is so widely dispersed, the literature review of each study serves as a critical point of integration, bringing together materials that readers—no matter how experienced they are in SoTL work—may not have previously encountered.

Researchers also bear a responsibility to the discipline of SoTL itself. Contextualizing work within the body of knowledge serves to strengthen the field and the network of connections among studies, theoretical and practical understandings, and disciplines and people. The literature review process and product serve to knit the field together. Incomplete, inadequate, or hasty reviews leave gaps and unravel the work of others. Work that follows and relies on these incomplete previous works becomes even less securely connected to the discipline, its tenuous assumptions incapable of bearing the weight of practice. SoTL as a field has been (rightly) criticized for the lack of rigor and depth in literature reviews (McKinney, 2010; Weimer, 2006), where often there are few links to theory or to relevant studies in other fields (Kanuka, 2011). From my librarian's perspective in reading SoTL work, it often seems that the researcher has made good use of the teaching knowledge base in her or his home discipline but has not extended the search process or the synthesized product to include work outside the researcher's field. It sometimes appears as though the literature review had been an afterthought, based on a cursory search to find papers that support the claims of a given study without much deep analysis of the quality of that prior work. The only way to answer those criticisms is for researchers to expand the range of their literature search process and write stronger reviews and for reviewers and publishers to encourage them in that work.

Considering literature reviews from a publishing standpoint brings up another practical reason to spend time on the process. Thorough literature reviews make publication more likely. In their study of reviews of articles Chick, Poole, and Blackman (2017) determined that the literature review was the most frequent target of feedback and reason for rejection or resubmission decisions. This concern is not unique to SoTL editors and reviewers; similar statements are found in editorials across academic disciplines and in wider studies of reviewing behavior (Raamkumar, Foo, & Pang, 2016).

The SoTL Literature Review as Process: Challenges and Approaches

There are particular challenges in conducting literature reviews in SoTL. SoTL work can be difficult to find efficiently, and the workflow of searching, identifying, assessing, and synthesizing prior work is complicated by the fact that most researchers will have to step outside their disciplinary comfort zones. A process that is familiar and easy in one's home discipline can feel dismayingly difficult in SoTL.

The literature that may inform SoTL work is diverse and dispersed across specialist SoTL publications, journals on teaching and learning, and discipline-focused publications. There is no single database that brings it all together, no established thesaurus of consistent terms. Although there are some key people (many of whom are contributors to this volume), there is no agreed-on canon of literature. A substantial amount of the work is in fact not published in a traditional manner but rather is available through conference proceedings, institutional websites, university repositories, and records of local professional development centers and sessions. Weimer (2006) illuminated the situation beautifully:

> Previously published work on teaching and learning looks more like a house cobbled together by many different occupants, all working without blueprints and very little money. That it stands at all is something of a wonder. But the neighborhood has changed, thanks to greater interest in teaching generally and the scholarship of teaching and learning specifically. Folks are moving in and calling this place their scholarly home. (p. 51)

These challenges call for a different approach to searching, an approach that may provoke discomfort. As Weller (2011) and Webb (2015) have noted, academics are often uncomfortable outside their own disciplines where they feel they are no longer experts. I often recommend that SoTL researchers get in touch with their inner undergraduates, a state Webb (2015) characterized as "studentness" (p. 108). This may entail searching by topics rather than by familiar names, sacrificing (at least at first) depth for breadth, experimenting with unfamiliar terminology, and casting a wider net to find materials that truly support the work. As Naylor advises in McKinney's (2010) key text on conducting SoTL, "Traditional database searching, while useful for locating peer-reviewed journal articles, will probably not prove to be as comprehensive as researchers may have come to expect when conducting research in other disciplines" (p. 37). Recalling the needs of the reader and the discipline, it is also useful to search for older material, even though disciplinary research may focus on current work. This is not a problem confined to SoTL: A journal editor wrote, "Failure to cite pioneering work robs the builders of our discipline of their just recognition and gives younger researchers a distorted and incomplete view of the development of the field" (Neuzil, 2004, p. 797).

Drinkwater and colleagues (2014) built connections among early and seminal work in higher education practice, active learning theory, and individual studies drawn mostly from physics. The sources included work from outside North America and were not limited to peer-reviewed journals but included books and reports from higher education institutions and organizations. The literature review is commendable for its breadth, drawing from more general works on teaching to build connections across disciplines.

In a field where there is no set terminology and no single repository of resources, how is it possible to search effectively? Move away from familiar disciplinary search engines like the Modern Language Association's International Bibliography or PubMed and switch to tools that search across the multidisciplinary landscape, such as Google Scholar, which also includes many sources that most proprietary databases don't index, including theses, open access publications, departmental websites, institutional repositories, conference materials, and guides for new faculty. Each institution's library may have a comprehensive tool that searches across books and subject specific databases, similar to Google Scholar, leading to sources researchers might otherwise miss, so it's useful to consult an institutional librarian early in the process. Their awareness of available indexes such as JSTOR (particularly good for the humanities) and Scopus (similarly useful for the sciences) and advanced search techniques can save a lot of time.

I recommend specific steps for searching Google Scholar to liberate researchers from disciplinary constraints in gathering information beyond the comfortable boundaries of home disciplines. Start with the aspect of learning under investigation, and then layer in terms for particular kinds of students. Only after seeing the breadth of studies available across the disciplines that could provide connections to protocols and theories with which I am less familiar would I use terms specific to the discipline. For example, if I was looking at whether group quizzes improved conceptual understanding in a freshman biology course, my Google Scholar search progression might look like the following: "group quizzes" "conceptual understanding" ("freshman or freshmen" or "first-year students") / "group quizzes" "conceptual understanding" ("freshman or freshmen" or "first-year students") "science."

Of course, this wouldn't be the only search I would perform. My process would include broad searches of the discipline, SoTL, and the teaching topic (e.g., biology SoTL "group quiz"), as well as searches with terms for particular theories, methods, and methodologies. Google Scholar will also identify useful books, often the best resources for the foundational work in SoTL or on particular methods and theories.

In searching the literature as part of the research method, a useful habit is recording databases and search terms as well as references, especially if SoTL work is just one aspect of a researcher's complex workload. It makes it easier to regularly update literature reviews and extend rather than repeat searches, especially in collaborative work. Other useful habits include noting key people and institutions as additional search terms, watching for potential dissemination venues, and checking for geographic gaps in search results. There is a lot of useful SoTL work being done in Nordic countries, South Africa, Singapore, and Australia that may be harder to find just because of slight variations in terminology. There is also a growing body of work in languages other than English.

Reviewing the literature doesn't, however, end at searching. Each relevant article may be a source of more resources through works cited in the article and through those that have cited it. Additionally, an often neglected resource in embarking on work in a new field is people. I advise tracking down authors and presenters through publications, conference programs, Twitter, and institutional or personal websites, and asking for introductions to other scholars. Contacting these other researchers may open up reams of research that might otherwise remain hidden.

For those not already using software to keep track of references and other important pieces of information, it may be useful to invest some time investigating the options. Institutions may subscribe to products like EndNote or Refworks, but there are also a number of freely available resources such as Zotero. Many libraries maintain lists that track new tools and compare features (e.g., www.lib.sfu.ca/find/research-tools/citation-software). Some tools, like Mendeley, are also searchable, providing another way into literature that has yielded some gems for me in the past. There are also some tools built into writing software, like Scrivener, and even Google Docs has the ability to track and insert references.

The SoTL Literature Review: From Process to Product

In SoTL work, finding the relevant literature is often the most technically difficult step. Writing the literature review, or creating the product, is also challenging in its own way. This feeling of returning to "studentness" (Webb, 2015, p. 108) can feel disorienting. Working with that literature, understanding the patterns, and synthesizing the work of researchers across diverse disciplines often require dealing with unfamiliar jargon, new methods, and uncertainty in drawing boundaries between what is and what isn't relevant.

Boutet, Vandette, and Valiquette-Tessier (2017) drew on work published across disciplinary and SoTL journals, including sources that support the benefits of reflection and those that do not. They also cited extensively from the research methods literature to support their choices in developing a protocol, coding, and analyzing their data, which is valuable to SoTL researchers who may use similar methods.

A number of SoTL literature reviews I've seen read more like annotated bibliographies, describing a few resources, and less like a reliable guide to the conversations that can inform conducting and interpreting a study. The challenge lies in finding a place for our own work in a field of study we don't yet completely understand. As we're not used to feeling unfamiliar in an academic context, this may manifest itself by our shutting down and writing a literature review piecemeal. This kind of review, though, suggests that we don't see the value in literature that doesn't speak our language or in teaching and learning in other contexts; this is a narrow view that can weaken our understanding of teaching and learning in general. In contrast, by widening our search, we draw threads together across the tapestry of academia, creating a richer picture of teaching and learning.

White and Nitkin's (2014) literature review provides a brief but thorough introduction to transformational pedagogy, outlining its history, recent development of the theory, its application, and its connections to critical pedagogy. Their literature review focuses on the bigger picture of the specific pedagogy in question and across a range of teaching contexts.

To illustrate, I include here my literature review for a major phenomenography project on students' reading of scholarly articles (see MacMillan, 2014). For my process, I found it helpful to keep a journal as I did my literature review. I recorded key points, quotations, and thoughts that occurred to me as I went through each source. Much of the analysis and synthesis occurred in a second phase required by my illegible handwriting. Every two or three days, I went through my journal and transcribed it in an online document. This review and transcription also allowed me to make connections to articles I read in the intervening time, bringing those articles into conversation with each other even before I started the formal synthesis work. I found it helpful to use different colors and fonts to distinguish these second thoughts, so when it came time to write the literature review I relied almost entirely on those brightly colored notes. As I was bringing materials together, I realized I needed to go back to the origins of the research approach I used. Reading about the evolution of phenomenography allowed me to incorporate my changing understanding of learning into my own work and led to further articles and books that found their way into my literature review. By the end, the product of my review documented a very diverse conversation among a wide range of sources, including works on reading in K–12 sectors and various academic disciplines, works on the neurobiology of reading, and theories of cognition and schema building. In turn, it made information available to readers who may not otherwise have found these sources and certainly wouldn't have seen them brought together. This literature review also contributed to the growing body of SoTL work on reading, serving as a staging ground for people who want to take the inquiry further.

A SoTL literature review that is useful to researchers, readers, and the discipline connects diverse disciplines, past and present, theory and practice. It brings together individual points of light from prior work into constellations that take on a meaning greater than the sum of their parts.

References

Boutet, I., Vandette, M. P., & Valiquette-Tessier, S. C. (2017). Evaluating the implementation and effectiveness of reflection writing. *Canadian Journal for the Scholarship of Teaching and Learning, 8*(1). Retrieved from http://ir.lib.uwo.ca/cjsotl_rcacea/vol8/iss1/8

Chick, N., Poole, G, & Blackman, G. (2017). *Peer review in the scholarship of teaching and learning.* Manuscript in preparation.

Drinkwater, M. J., Gannaway, D., Sheppard, K., Davis, M. J., Wegener, M. J., Bowen, W. P., & Corney, J. F. (2014). Managing active learning processes in large first year physics classes: The advantages of an integrated approach. *Teaching & Learning Inquiry, 2*(2), 75–90. Retrieved from http://tlijournal.com/tli/index.php/TLI/article/view/73

Hutchings, P., Huber, M. T., & Ciccone, A. (2011). *The scholarship of teaching and learning reconsidered: Institutional integration and impact.* San Francisco, CA: Jossey-Bass.

Kanuka, H. (2011). Keeping the scholarship in the scholarship of teaching and learning. *International Journal for the Scholarship of Teaching and Learning, 5*(1), 1–12. Retrieved from http://digitalcommons.georgiasouthern.edu/ij-sotl/vol5/iss1/3/

MacMillan, M. (2014). Student connections with academic texts: A phenomenographic study of reading. *Teaching in Higher Education, 19,* 943–954.

McKinney, K. (2010). *Enhancing learning through the scholarship of teaching and learning: The challenges and joys of juggling.* Boston, MA: Anker.

Miller-Young, J., & Yeo, M. (2015). Conceptualizing and communicating SoTL: A framework for the field. *Teaching and Learning Inquiry, 3*(2), 37–53.

Neuzil, C. E. (2004). Nothing older than three years. *Ground Water, 42,* 797–798.

Raamkumar, A. S., Foo, S., & Pang, N. (2016). Survey on inadequate and omitted citations in manuscripts: A precursory study in identification of tasks for a literature review and manuscript writing assistive system. *Information Research, 21*(4). Retrieved from http://www.informationr.net/ir/21-4/paper733.html

Savory, P., Burnett, A., & Goodburn, A. M. (2007). *Inquiry into the college classroom: A journey toward scholarly teaching.* Boston, MA: Anker.

Webb, A. S. (2015). *Threshold concepts in the scholarship of teaching and learning: A phenomenological study of educational leaders in a Canadian research-intensive university.* Retrieved from https://open.library.ubc.ca/cIRcle/collections/24/items/1.0167152

Weimer, M. (2006). *Enhancing scholarly work on teaching and learning: Professional literature that makes a difference*. San Francisco, CA: Jossey-Bass.

Weller, S. (2011). New lecturers' accounts of reading higher education research. *Studies in Continuing Education, 33*(1), 93–106.

White, S. K., & Nitkin, M. R. (2014). Creating a transformational learning experience: Immersing students in an intensive interdisciplinary learning environment. *International Journal for the Scholarship of Teaching and Learning, 8*(2), 1–30.

4

EDUCATIONAL RESEARCH AND SoTL

Converging in the Commons

Kimberley A. Grant

Whereas educational research has traditionally been the province of faculty in schools or departments of education, or education specialists in some disciplines, the scholarship of teaching and learning invites involvement by faculty across the full spectrum of research specialties and fields. (Huber & Hutchings, 2006, p. 30)

Although it can lead to some confusion and awkward moments, there are certain benefits to being a latecomer to an ongoing conversation. Although we each bring to any conversation our own perspectives and "prejudices," which is Gadamer's (1989, p. 273) preferred term for our linguistic, historic, and cultural lenses, newcomers are less likely to be aware of the undercurrents and tensions already at play. We may naively ask questions that insiders would avoid, and we may be excused for blundering into sensitive topics because we genuinely don't know any better. In a sense, this was my experience when, as a new graduate student in educational research, I stumbled my way into a growing familiarity with the field of the scholarship of teaching and learning (SoTL).

It all started with a conference. I had been told that I should be attending academic conferences to become familiar with this mode of disseminating research. A Google search led me to an event that sounded promising: it was all about teaching and learning, which seemed appropriate for someone in educational research, and it was only an hour drive from my home. The registration deadline had already passed, but a short phone call to a helpful administrator led a friend and me to attend a preconference workshop and the first keynote address. Thus it was that I found myself at a SoTL conference with absolutely no idea what SoTL was.

That first introduction to SoTL was eye-opening and a little confusing. The big ideas resonated strongly with my own teaching experience and the kind of research I wanted to do, but the language, perspectives, and key names were unfamiliar. I tend to be a sit-back-and-watch-closely-before-jumping-in kind of person, so I tried to figure out what exactly this conference was all about through listening and observing. During the workshop, I was thrilled to hear a chemistry professor declare his commitment to improving student learning, but I was puzzled when he questioned the validity of doing classroom research to inform his teaching practice. As an experienced educator and novice educational researcher, I struggled to understand his objections. In the same way, I was pleasantly surprised by the warm welcome of the other participants and a little taken aback by their reactions to my introduction.

"Hi, I'm Kim. I'm a grad student."
"That's great!" came the kind replies. "What field are you in?"
"Education."
"Oh."

For some reason, that answer seemed to bring conversations to a halt, not because people were unfriendly but because they seemed a bit surprised. That day I met people in journalism, biology, chemistry, psychology, and history but no other educational researchers. Some of those who welcomed me did say it was unusual to have someone from education in attendance. "This must all be old hat for you," one chuckled, almost apologetically. I didn't know what to make of their comments. As a newcomer to SoTL and still a newcomer to educational research, almost nothing I encountered in academia seemed old hat to me. At dinner that evening, I spotted two familiar faces from my home department of education, but I remained puzzled that there were so very few of us in attendance at a nearby event focused on teaching and learning. Isn't that what educational research is all about?

Educational Research and SoTL as Contested Spaces

Since that first experience (about four years ago), I've had several opportunities to explore SoTL as a field and as a practice. I have a bit better understanding of its history, aims, and tensions. However, I am still a newcomer who sometimes asks awkward questions and experiences feelings of disequilibrium because SoTL includes both the familiar and the unfamiliar. One thing that continues to give me pause is the uneasiness I sense in the relationship between SoTL and educational research. Perhaps this tension is a sign of academic courtesy, with neither field wanting to infringe on the other's space. It may also be that researchers in both fields aren't always very familiar with the aims and practices of the other, and direct conversations are rare. Whatever the reason for this tension, I do sometimes find myself wanting to play the role of intermediary and introduce SoTL to educational researchers who should find much of the research interesting and enlightening and to describe the breadth of educational research to those in SoTL who may only have encountered quantitative educational methodologies.

Just yesterday, a friend and colleague in educational research and I were discussing SoTL and comparing the challenges of doing classroom-based action research in K–12 schools and in higher education settings. While we were talking about how SoTL researchers have the added difficulty of obtaining ethics approval, she admitted, "I still feel a little confused about this whole thing. I mean, isn't SoTL what we in educational research have been doing all along? Is it really something new and different?" She posed this as a sincere question, but I have also heard the notion of SoTL as just another name for educational research conveyed with an eye roll. In the midst of a group discussion on teaching strategies for large classes, one of the only other education specialists in the room rolled her eyes and said, "We have known this stuff forever!" Ah, I thought, *this* is where that old hat comment came from. Clearly some do assume that SoTL research is retracing well-worn paths through the fields of teaching and learning that educational researchers have already paved.

Perhaps it is in response to this sense of "We were here first" that some SoTL researchers choose to deal directly with what might be perceived as contested space between SoTL and educational research. Geertsema (2016) highlights the problems that arise for academics when SoTL is "conflated with educational research" (p. 126) and warns that it is neither realistic nor helpful to expect disciplinary experts to also "develop a parallel expertise in education" (p. 127) prior to studying teaching and learning in their own contexts. Instead, he argues, SoTL should be positioned as more of a practice than a field of research. Others, however, would disagree and position educational research as a disciplinary ancestor that can provide theoretical grounding for SoTL as a research field (e.g., Miller-Young & Yeo, 2015). The implication of this parental relationship, however, is that SoTL must branch out to establish its independence. Still other studies place SoTL and educational research on a continuum in which SoTL is the gateway to the real work of educational research (Streveler, Borrego, & Smith, 2007). This seems to be an issue of numerous positions and ongoing debates.

Such assumptions on both sides, though, may hinder the rich exchange of discovery and insights from both modes of inquiry. As a newcomer, it seems to me that the relationship between educational research and SoTL is like many other apparent tensions within the scope of teaching and learning. As Biesta (2010) says of other educational debates, this is "not an issue that can be 'fixed' but one that requires ongoing conversation" (p. 117). Entering these ongoing conversations, as I mentioned before, can feel awkward. It is helpful, though, to remember that each of our first disciplines also has contested and contestable topics that were once new to us. Remembering that we don't need to become experts in everything before taking first steps and that our own disciplinary expertise provides the necessary lens for us to take a closer look at teaching and learning in our discipline-specific classrooms can provide the confidence we need as we begin to engage with the language and practices of educational research and SoTL.

Avoiding Another Enclosure Movement

A familiar metaphor in SoTL is the image of the "big tent" (Huber & Hutchings, 2005, p. 4), but it is not always clear whether educational research is considered to be under the SoTL tent, or if it is the other way around. More recently, the language of fields has become prominent, particularly in conversations about the relationship between educational research and SoTL as well as with educational development (Clegg, 2012; Geertsema, 2016; Kenny et al., 2017). Questions arise, therefore, about where and how to build the fences between these academic fields. I am drawn to the idea of conceptualizing areas of inquiry as fields but am concerned that these kinds of questions might lead to a kind of teaching and learning enclosure movement.

Throughout the Middle Ages and beyond, common grazing and farming lands across western Europe and particularly in England were fenced off "into the carefully delineated and individually owned and managed farm plots of modern times" ("Enclosure," 1998). This process of enclosure is supposed to have led to increased food production because of innovation and the industrialization of agricultural practices. These changes, however, also marked the end of communal farming and cooperation among landholders and agricultural workers. Debates have resurfaced about just how much this cause-and-effect relationship can be assumed, and how much food production would have increased without enclosure and privatization (Boyle, 2007). My concern about the enclosure of fields in teaching and learning is not as much about ownership rights and intellectual property (although that is an important concern; see Huber & Hutchings, 2006) as it is about the free circulation of researchers and ideas from different perspectives and scholarly traditions related to teaching and learning.

Earlier in SoTL's history there was a call for the cultivation of a teaching commons that welcomed all kinds of disciplinary experts (Huber & Hutchings, 2005). Research into teaching and learning in higher education, it was proposed, had already been carried on in fragmented and privatized ways, and it would be crucial "to faculty and students [and] to all who care about the quality of higher education and its larger social role" (Huber & Hutchings, 2005, p. 7) to develop and protect a commons of teaching and learning—opening up spaces rather than fencing them off. I experienced a taste of this kind of commons at that first SoTL conference. Academics from a host of disciplinary backgrounds shared their questions, resources, and research in ways that allowed pedagogy to take "center stage" (Huber & Hutchings, 2005, p. 7). However, I wonder if there is an ongoing tension between the desire for a teaching and learning commons and the same enclosure impulse that originally led postsecondary teachers to work behind "doors that are both metaphorically and physically closed to colleagues" (Huber & Hutchings, 2006, p. 26). Even as academic teaching is coming out from behind closed disciplinary doors, there may still be (to mix my metaphors) a desire to build and strengthen fences among the multiple avenues of research that support teaching and learning including educational research, SoTL, and educational development.

From the perspective of higher education research, Clegg (2012) raises important questions about how to conceptualize the notion of a field and wonders "whether there are related fields: research into higher education, academic development and disciplinary teaching research, rather than one" (p. 667). I propose that it may be helpful to think of it as a single field—teaching and learning—and to consider that there are many ways of working with and in that field. My understanding of the concept of a field of knowledge has been deeply shaped by my educational research background including the work of scholars such as Friesen and Jardine (2009). The following refers to mathematics as the field in question, but I wonder if it might provide some new insight if we substitute teaching and learning for mathematics:

> We are convinced that, as a living landscape or field, that field has within it a great range of diversity, multiplicity, modes and forms and figures. It has an elaborate ancestry of work and works, traces and tracks. As such, as a living field, mathematics is amenable to a wide range of explorers . . . and interests, strengths and forgivable weaknesses, *because this is in the nature of a living field.* (Friesen & Jardine, 2009, p. 156, emphasis in original)

Friesen and Jardine (2009) speak of mathematics as a living landscape because long before people thought to study and teach mathematics formally, mathematical knowledge and practice were active in the world. In other words, we do not study mathematics in schools because people need to add math to the world; we study mathematics because it is already a part of the world.

I would like to propose that in a similar way the field of teaching and learning has been a living (and lively) landscape long before anyone sought to study it in either K–12 or higher education contexts.

If we conceive of a field in this strongly metaphoric sense as a preexisting topography, then we can enter that field from many directions—through educational research, SoTL, educational development, the learning sciences, and others. Because a "living field *is* diverse" and "amenable to a wide range of explorers" (Friesen & Jardine, 2009, p. 156, emphasis in original), if we think of teaching and learning as this kind of field, there may be less of a need to parse the boundaries between these different modes of inquiry and more opportunities to benefit from multiple perspectives. This way of engaging with teaching and learning may also protect the field as a commons that enables research to be shared in a collaborative way that does not concern itself with hierarchies or who was where first.

To push the metaphor one step further, perhaps we can think of those who engage in these various approaches to the study of teaching and learning as not just explorers in the same field but as neighboring communities in the same landscape. I wonder if taking this kind of view may help us newcomers find our way into the field without feeling that we need to have everything figured out before we become involved.

Hutchings (2000), a proponent of a teaching commons, envisioned

Bass (1999) opened with an excerpt by Loewenberg Ball and Lampert, two prominent educational researchers who focus on teacher education and mathematics education. Although Bass focused on his own teaching experience in a higher educational setting, his honest description of a crisis in his classroom will resonate with teachers from a variety of contexts, illustrating the internally motivated desire to better understand how teaching affects student learning.

Case (2013) described how she began researching the impact of her race and gender courses long before she had heard of SoTL. Case started her own inquiry by using the disciplinary concerns of women's studies and the educational practice of pre- and posttesting to help her make adjustments to deepen student learning. Only later did she recognize that she was already working in the field of SoTL.

a positive, mutually beneficial relationship among those who study teaching and learning:

> Indeed these communities . . . enrich one another. [SoTL] may open up new questions that, over time, prompt major new lines of educational research. Educational research may suggest models and strategies that can be explored in the scholarship of teaching and learning and in scholarly teaching practice. (p. 9)

These kinds of synergistic possibilities seem to hold much more promise for the future of SoTL and educational research than the establishment of rigid boundaries. Approaching other research and researchers as neighbors from a nearby community rather than from the other (wrong?) side of the fence is more likely to lead to mutual enrichment. Considering research about teaching and learning, whether it comes from the perspective of educational researcher or educational development or SoTL, as potentially helpful to our own SoTL inquiries can expand the breadth and depth of possibilities for those inquiries.

Some Small Examples of Living in the Field

After that first SoTL conference experience, I continued to think about a chemistry professor who wanted to make changes in his teaching practice but was not sure where to start. I had just completed a literature review on teacher self-assessment practices and resources for my dissertation, and I began to wonder if some of the resources developed by educational researchers for K–12 teacher self-assessment (e.g., inventories and reflection questions on different aspects of practice) might also be helpful for postsecondary instructors. I put together a proposal for the next SoTL conference and presented my ideas on how self-assessment resources might provide vocabulary and focus for instructors who want to look more closely at their teaching and possibly begin SoTL research. The educational developers in attendance gladly took copies of the resources, and several said that although the exact versions may not be a perfect fit for university professors, they could likely adapt them or use them as conversation starters. Because learning to reflect on one's teaching is always a challenge, having some concrete self-assessment tools might support those who wonder what kinds of things they might reflect on. I don't know how or if any of those resources have been put to use, but having the opportunity to introduce new possibilities from educational research that "may suggest [new] models and strategies that can be explored" (Hutchings, 2000, p. 9) made me feel like a good neighbor.

Likewise, I have had many opportunities to draw on SoTL research and theorizing in the educational research community. For example, my home department uses the language of *signature pedagogies* in some program descriptions. Most of my education colleagues are unfamiliar with this term and with Shulman's (2005) work, so I have had the pleasure of providing introductions. In my own classes, I have also found it useful to draw on the work of Brookfield (1995) when I discuss the value of reflective practice with my preservice teaching students. Being able to see and investigate pedagogical approaches such as understanding by design (UbD; Wiggins & McTighe, 2005) from educational research and SoTL perspectives has deepened my ability to understand the benefits and drawbacks of UbD. In fact, UbD is a good example of an approach to teaching and learning that is equally applicable to K–12 and higher educational settings. I have found that the work of educational philosophers such as Biesta (2014) and learning psychologists such as Dweck (2008) also transcend the boundaries of different research approaches to teaching and learning and reassure me that it is not too idealistic to conceive of teaching and learning as a single living and diverse field that provides multiple entry points for those of us taking our first SoTL steps.

My examples serve not so much as role models for how this work of mutual enrichment ought to be done but instead as encouragement that it can be done. Educational research and SoTL do not need to jockey for position or negotiate contested spaces, and we newcomers do

Although Bass (1999) and Case (2013) drew on educational research ideas in their SoTL work, Roberts-Harris (2014) grounded her educational research work in SoTL principles. She chose to position her study as SoTL because the emphasis is on her particular context: "I believe knowledge and understanding gained through careful investigation of my teaching practices and my students' learning will ultimately benefit my students" (p. 94). That common motivation of benefiting students transcends different contexts and modes of educational inquiry.

As Haugnes and Russell (2016) emphasized in their description of a project to support rubric-based assessment in an art and design university, drawing on literature from "several fields" (p. 250) including SoTL, higher education, and K–12 education has enriched their work. Each lens contributes to a deeper understanding of the challenges and possibilities for teachers and learners.

not need to worry about whether we have strayed into one field from the other. Instead, we can enter the field of teaching and learning through our own gateways of research and inquiry and, once there, begin to find ways to learn from each other for the greater good of our students.

References

Bass, R. (1999). The scholarship of teaching: What's the problem? *Inventio, 1*(1), 1–10. Retrieved from https://my.vanderbilt.edu/sotl/files/2013/08/Bass-Problem1.pdf

Biesta, G. (2010). A brief response to Ton Jörg's review of good education in an age of measurement: Ethics, politics, democracy. *Complicity: An International Journal of Complexity and Education, 8*, 117–120.

Biesta, G. (2014). *The beautiful risk of education*. Boulder, CO: Paradigm.

Boyle, J. (2007). The second enclosure movement. *Renewal, 15*(4), 17–24.

Brookfield, S. (1995). *Becoming a critically reflective teacher*. San Francisco, CA: Jossey-Bass.

Case, K. A. (2013). Expanding the teaching commons: Making the case for a new perspective on SoTL. *InSight, 8*, 37–43. Retrieved from http://insightjournal.park.edu/wp-content/uploads/2015/08/Ch.-3-Faculty-Article-Expanding-the-Teaching-Commons-Making-the-Case-for-a-New-Perspective-on-SoTL.pdf

Clegg, S. (2012). Conceptualising higher education research and/or academic development as "fields": A critical analysis. *Higher Education Research & Development, 31*, 667–678. doi:10.1080/07294360.2012.690369

Dweck, C. S. (2008). *Mindset: The new psychology of success*. New York, NY: Ballantine Books.

Enclosure. (1998). In *Encylopaedia Brittanica*. Retrieved from www.britannica.com/topic/enclosure

Friesen, S., & Jardine, D. W. (2009). On field(ing) knowledge. In B. Sriraman & S. Goodchild (Eds.), *Relatively and philosophically E(a)rnest: Festschrift in honor of Paul Ernest's 65th birthday* (pp. 147–172). Charlotte, NC: Information Age.

Gadamer, H.-G. (1989). *Truth and method* (2nd rev.). New York, NY: Continuum.

Geertsema, J. (2016). Academic development, SoTL and educational research. *International Journal for Academic Development, 21*, 122–134. doi:10.1080/1360144X.2016.1175144

Haugnes, N., & Russell, J. L. (2016). Don't box me in: Rubrics for artists and designers. *To Improve the Academy, 35*, 249–283. doi:10.1002/tia2.20043

Huber, M. T., & Hutchings, P. (2005). *The advancement of learning: Building the learning commons*. San Francisco, CA: Jossey-Bass.

Huber, M. T., & Hutchings, P. (2006). Building the teaching commons. *Change, 38*(3), 24–31.

Hutchings, P. (2000). Introduction: Approaching the scholarship of teaching and learning. In P. Hutchings (Ed.), *Opening lines: Approaches to the scholarship of teaching and learning* (pp. 1–10). Menlo Park, CA: Carnegie Foundation for the Advancement of Teaching.

Kenny, N., Popovic, C., McSweeney, J., Knorr, K., Hoessler, C., Hall, S., . . . El Khoury, E. (2017). Drawing on the principles of SoTL to illuminate a path forward for the scholarship of educational development. *Canadian Journal for the Scholarship of Teaching and Learning, 8*(2), 1–17.

Miller-Young, J., & Yeo, M. (2015). Conceptualizing and communicating SoTL: A framework for the field. *Teaching & Learning Inquiry, 3*(2), 37–53. doi: 10.20343/teachlearninqu.3.2.37

Roberts-Harris, D. (2014). What did they take away? Examining newly qualified U.S. teachers' visions of learning and teaching science in K–8 classrooms. *Teaching & Learning Inquiry, 2*, 91–107. Retrieved from http://tlijournal.com/tli/index.php/TLI/article/view/78/47

Shulman, L. S. (2005). Signature pedagogies in the professions. *Daedalus, 134*(3), 52–59. doi:10.1162/0011526054622015

Streveler, R. A., Borrego, M., & Smith, K. A. (2007). Moving from the "scholarship of teaching and learning" to "educational research": An example from engineering. *To Improve the Academy, 25*, 139–149.

Wiggins, G., & McTighe, J. (2005). *Understanding by design* (2nd ed.). Alexandria, VA: Association for Supervision and Curriculum Development.

5

IDENTIFYING A TRADITION OF INQUIRY

Articulating Research Assumptions

Carol Berenson

My disciplinary pathway into educational development comes by way of philosophy, sociology, and women's studies, so when I first ventured into the scholarship of teaching and learning (SoTL) terrain, it was exciting to encounter scholars from multiple disciplines investigating student learning by drawing on their specific traditions of research and teaching. However, despite claims to welcome multiple perspectives into the "big tent" (Huber & Hutchings, 2005, p. 4), the terrain is also rich with discussions about positioning certain approaches to SoTL research as more credible and rigorous than others (Chick, 2014; Potter & Wuetherick, 2015). Sociologists would call this a strategic site from which to learn about a field, as the very foundations of what research is all about are robustly debated in the context of this "salad" bar of possibilities (Poole, 2012, p. 137). This presents challenges and opportunities for emerging SoTL researchers.

In order to claim a space as a legitimate SoTL practitioner, it is helpful to do some preliminary thinking about the assumptions underlying our approach to research or our research paradigm. In our own disciplines, assumptions often go unacknowledged. However, awareness of our research paradigm helps us see and defend for others the rigor of our work, including the logical progression of what counts as evidence, how we generate and analyze that evidence, and the claims we make about the broader relevance of our research when all is said and done (Mason, 1996). Feminists have taught us that all research comes from a place of assumptions about its purpose, the social world, and knowledge (Harding, 1991), and that some approaches have been privileged over others by not having to acknowledge their underpinnings. For example, feminist critics have long revealed biases inherent in the metaphors of so-called objective science that serve to privilege White European masculinity as the ideal (Fox Keller, 1985; Martin, 1992). As the SoTL debates make clear, when paradigmatic assumptions are not uncovered and articulated, all research is held up to the same standards— those of the dominant paradigm. This can position some research as not research at all. When different traditions are acknowledged and understood, we embrace alternative language and standards to talk about and evaluate our work. By laying out our research paradigm or the fundamental assumptions we bring to a project, we can articulate the rigor and legitimacy of our research to ourselves and to a broader SoTL audience.

A Positivist–Constructivist Continuum

For this discussion, the contrast between positivism and constructivism provides a useful frame to understand important differences between long-standing research traditions and their underlying assumptions. My intention is not to create a false dichotomy or to oversimplify by suggesting that all research is reducible to two distinct and homogeneous categories. Rather, positivism and constructivism are best understood as representing the farthest endpoints along a continuum of possibilities. (Many such continuums exist in the literature, e.g., Miller-Young & Yeo [2015] discuss a six-point scale.) For the present purposes then, I paint positivism and constructivism with broad strokes to highlight them as traditions of inquiry that can help us to appreciate key differences and where our own research inclinations lie. Additionally, while recognizing a power differential here, I don't intend to position one paradigm over the other; rather, both are valuable in terms of understanding student learning. However, given that constructivists are the most likely to be challenged on the SoTL landscape, this chapter is intended to provide tools and insights particularly for those who find themselves at this end of the spectrum speaking back to those at the other end.

Methodology to Method: A Logical Progression

A distinction between methodology and method is helpful here. Methodology involves the assumptions or beliefs underlying our research that shape and justify the logic of how we approach a study, such as the assumption that the researcher should be a neutral, invisible entity in the research process. Methods, which flow from our methodology, are the tools we use to gather or analyze data, such as the standardized surveys or exams that would best

TABLE 5.1
Comparing Positivist and Constructivist Paradigms

Positivist Paradigm	Constructivist Paradigm
Objective point of view (one knowable, external reality to be accurately described by the researcher)	Subjective point of view (multiple perceived or interpreted realities to be examined by the researcher)
Replicable, value-free inquiry by an invisible researcher	Emergent, value-bound inquiry by a situated researcher
Deductive logic or hypothesis testing	Inductive logic or theory building
Methods include standardized surveys, scales, interviews	Methods include a conversation with a purpose, active interview
Numerical data and statistical analysis	Text-based data and thematic analysis
Findings are empirically generalizable	Findings are theoretically generalizable

Note. Adapted from Hamilton & Schonwetter (2015).

fit with this assumption of researcher invisibility and neutrality. Table 5.1 and the discussion that follows move from the theoretical (methodology) to the practical (method), much like our process of conducting a study might progress.

Foundational Beliefs About Knowledge and Reality: Objective or Subjective Point of View

A good place to begin is by reflecting on our tradition's beliefs about what counts as reality and knowledge of it. At the heart of positivism are the researcher's assumptions of an objective point of view and a real world out there to be accurately described. For example, when researchers talk about their findings, it is indicative of this positivist assumption about an external reality that is there to be discovered or found. With an agenda to discover the truth of this external reality, positivistic research typically embraces the experimental method as the most logical way to conduct inquiry into the natural or social world (Bryman, 2001). Tellingly referred to as *the* scientific method, this approach is frequently implemented to address questions of "what works?" (Hutchings, 2000, p. 4) in the context of SoTL research. Such a project might involve comparing student learning across two different groups, one of which experienced an intervention (e.g., an inquiry-based approach) and one of which did not. Assuming all else to be the same between the two groups, the researcher can then conclude that the inquiry-based approach has or has not worked in terms of student learning. It is interesting to note that, in this What works? research context where learning is objectively measured and compared, students are positioned as test subjects who are either right or wrong according to an outside, objective measure of learning.

In contrast, constructivist researchers posit that perceptions and interpretations of reality are the relevant knowledge to be gleaned through research. To be clear, constructivists don't deny the existence of a world of material objects (e.g., textbooks) or external phenomena (e.g., student learning). However, what is relevant and researchable for them about a phenomenon like student learning are the descriptions, perceptions, and interpretations that students assign to it. Hutchings's (2000) SoTL question of "What is?" (p. 4) is often best addressed through the logic of a constructivist approach where there is not one truth to be discovered (Does it work?), but rather a messy and complicated terrain to be uncovered and made sense of (How does it work?). Rather than comparing, here the project might investigate the question of how learning works in an inquiry-based classroom by delving deeply into the complexities of learning as experienced through the eyes of the students. In contrast to a positivist approach, in this What is? research context, students are positioned as research participants who are experts in their own experience. Researchers are tasked with capturing the subjective, perceived, interpreted realities of learning rather than measuring and assessing learning as either right or wrong.

Researcher's Role: Value-Free/Value-Bound Inquiry

As another methodological concern, positivism sees research as an objective, value-free endeavor that constitutes a view from nowhere. Good research is ideally free of bias, and the researcher should not be relevant or visible in the project. The idea that research can be replicated or identically repeated because it is neutrally conducted is a key aspect of positivist thinking (standardized surveys or exams can be administered by anyone in any setting). Our SoTL experiment on inquiry-based learning takes replication as fundamental when two different student groups of research subjects are separately exposed to the same assessments (e.g., surveys or exams) for comparative purposes.

In keeping with constructivist assumptions, Kalin (2012) described himself as "not a disinterested participant" (p. 8), illustrating the situated researcher's narrative in a project that involves an emergent design, an active interviewing style, and an inductive data analysis.

Additionally, the entire experiment is expected to able to be repeated or replicated in another setting with similar or identical results.

However, constructivists argue that all research operates from a set of assumptions, and that the researcher's interests inevitably shape the project at hand. There is no objective research, so rather than seeing the researcher's assumptions as a potential source of bias, such concerns simply ground all projects. The research design is more emergent than replicable because situated and visible researchers reflect on their impact and assumptions, and respond and orient to research participants according to the participants' agendas and concerns (more on this later). Rather than claim value-free methods and replicability as indicative of rigor, transparency and reflexivity about one's assumptions, interests, and decisions throughout the research process constitute rigor in many constructivist paradigms.

In Manarin (2012), transparency is front and center as she made explicit her assumptions and interests in the topic at hand and described in detail her methodological moves and decisions along the way.

Research Design: Deductive/Inductive Logic

Moving to the level of methods, within a positivist What works? frame, the logic of hypothesis testing is front and center. Our SoTL experiment might hypothesize that inquiry-based group learning activities will lead to the achievement of higher order learning outcomes than traditional lecture-based learning. This hypothesis is then tested by comparing pre- and post-assessments of two groups exposed to different sets of learning activities, and different findings can be deduced to be attributable to the activities (if, as previously mentioned, all other possible differences between the groups are controlled for). In other words, the deductive flow of logic begins with a theory (or hypothesis), and then the researcher gathers data to test it.

In contrast, inductive logic makes sense for constructivists given their underlying assumptions about reality as constructed and mediated through the interpretive work of researchers and their study participants. For a constructivist working within a What is? framework, the logical flow would begin with the data, and from there concepts or theories would be subsequently produced. For instance, in our inquiry-based study, the researcher might begin with interviews with students (or learning journals or think-alouds) to find out what is most relevant to their learning from the participants' perspectives. These data might reveal that group dynamics are an important feature of the learning experience that need to be more deeply investigated and then theorized. A different line of questioning might be implemented in subsequent interviews to explore this emerging theme. The logic of a bottom-up, data-to-theory approach once again lends itself to a flexible research design as patterns emerging from the data might suggest a shift in the researcher's emphasis or plan. Rigor is about demonstrating to others that one's research has been carefully planned, intentionally implemented, and is responsive to its participants by following their lead rather than a predetermined researcher's agenda.

Standardized Surveys, Scales, Interviews: A Conversation With a Purpose

Because positivism calls for standardized, replicable data collection methods, often surveys or scales are administered in which participants select from a predetermined set of options or categories designed to test the hypothesis. A positivist approach might also involve asking more open-ended questions on a survey or in an interview setting; however, the requirement of standardization and replication dictates a structured question-and-answer format with the researcher remaining as invisible as possible. In our SoTL study, a survey might be administered twice to each group of students, initially to measure their baseline knowledge and then subsequently their end-of-term knowledge. Structured interviews could also be conducted at the end of the term with representative groups of students from each of the lecture-based and inquiry-based classes to capture key differences between the groups. Whether the questions are closed- or open-ended, the language of the questions aims to have objective, clear meanings as posed and intended by the researcher. This illustrates a key concern for positivist researchers—the issue of validity, or the question of whether the researchers are studying what they set out to study. Rigor is about ensuring that one's research instruments are in fact valid, and considerable testing of instruments typically occurs to deal with this concern.

The constructivist agenda to capture the experiences of participants requires a flexible method such as a conversation with a purpose (Burgess, 1998). Rather than a positivist vessel-of-answers approach in which the researcher is accessing answers to questions that somehow preexist in the interviewee, the interview is considered a collaborative meaning-making event between the interviewer and interviewee. At the end of the constructivist continuum lies the active interview (Holstein & Gubrium, 2002) in which the researcher is highly engaged with the participant in a mutual act of constructing and interpreting knowledge (or data). By sharing thoughts, ideas, interpretations, and conclusions as they occur, the active interviewer offers participants the opportunity to correct, interpret, and actually begin the analytic process during the conversation. In our SoTL study, open-ended interviews might be conducted with student volunteers who come forward because they have something to say about the teaching approach, which would provide the impetus for the discussion guide loosely followed by the researcher. As the interviews progress, the interviewer might pick up on and follow new directions or refer to previous interview discussions to deepen or clarify the issues at hand. Although positivists would see the researcher as influencing the conversation in this approach, sharing power in a two-way exchange can lead to a rich account of students' learning experiences from a constructivist perspective. Finally, rather than a positivist concern about validity (Am I actually studying what I set out to study?), this approach regards authenticity (Do the participants see themselves represented in the data and analysis?) as the gold standard. Constructivist researchers often provide participants with transcripts (and sometimes analysis documents) so the participants can ascertain whether their voices and experiences have been appropriately represented (and interpreted) by the researcher.

Data Analysis: Statistical Analysis of Numerical Data/Thematic Analysis of Text-Based Data

Positivist approaches involve producing numerical data to make statistical analyses possible. A simple example from our SoTL experiment involves calculating an average final exam score for each of the student groups and then comparing across the groups to determine what works best, the inquiry-based or lecture-based learning. Statistical approaches allow us to summarize data from a large number of participants (which is typically required), making powerful descriptions, comparisons, and predictions possible.

In contrast, constructivists typically rely on text-based data (transcripts of interviews or think-aloud sessions or reflective journals) they analyze through close reading and iterative coding. Transcripts might be coded, thematized, carved up, or "bagged," (Mason, 1996, p. 129) for analysis across cases and data placed into similar categories that eventually become dominant patterns and themes. This does not mean that data are never quantified in constructivist approaches because counting the instances of the codes in a promising evolving theme might well be required to see if it is, in fact,

In Woolf's (2017) autoethnography, the reflexive researcher is highly visible, and a strong constructivist voice is evident, particularly in the data analysis section.

predominant in the data. In our inquiry-based classroom, the importance of group work might become a dominant theme as coding takes place across a series of interviews. Constructivists might also code data with an eye toward identifying unique or important insights pertaining to the phenomenon being explored, even if these insights are not dominant. This would make counting irrelevant and researchers' transparency and reflexivity important because their interests (or biases) and scholarly insights might shape what matters in the final analysis. For instance, one student's experience of and reflections on the impact of peer teaching in the inquiry-based classroom might be flagged as an insightful and important point by our SoTL researcher. Alternatively, at times data are examined using a more holistic approach that does not make comparisons across cases but rather looks in cases for themes or processes. The type of study being conducted will ultimately determine how data are coded and made sense of by the researcher, and once again, being explicit about one's assumptions at the beginning will lead to eventual decisions about coding and analysis. Rather than reducing variation by calculating and comparing average scores, constructivists consider complexity and messiness as a given in their approaches to data analysis, which is not seen as a problem; in fact it is a strength for qualitative research aimed at ascertaining what is. Exploring and analyzing learning as a complicated, messy endeavor allows constructivists to delve deeply into the nuances of how learning works and what it looks like.

Drawing Conclusions: Empirically/Theoretically Generalizable

Finally, and perhaps most important, we come to the issue of what kinds of larger claims can be made about the relevance of our specific research projects. The logic of a quantitative positivist approach allows empirical generalizability. This means that if carried out according to the standards of good quantitative research we can generalize the findings of our research from a smaller group, or representative sample of students, to a larger group, or the population the representative sample is drawn from. For instance, our SoTL study might conclude that statistically speaking inquiry-based learning does in fact lead to higher order learning outcomes than traditional lecture-based learning for a majority of students. Interestingly, large SoTL studies seldom draw participants from a population beyond the classrooms in question, which means the studies are not technically empirically generalizable. However, they are often seen as such simply by virtue of the number of participants involved in the study, and those conducting studies with large numbers of participants are seldom asked to clarify or justify their conclusions.

Although qualitative constructivist research typically involves smaller numbers of participants, this does not mean that it is idiosyncratic, anecdotal, or purely local. The types of larger claims that are made about constructivist research simply need to align with the assumptions and logic of these approaches rather than with those of their positivist counterparts. When qualitative researchers talk about the limitations of their studies in terms of a small number of participants, they are responding to their positivist counterparts and reinforcing misunderstandings about methodological differences between the two groups. Unlike positivists, constructivist agendas involve deeply exploring and investigating the complexities and nuances of the experiences, perspectives, and learnings of the students they purposefully rather than randomly choose as research participants. There is no attempt to summarize numerically through calculating averages or to objectively (by controlling for variation when possible) compare and contrast representative groups of participants. Rather, a qualitative constructivist approach involves carving out a thin slice of experience and digging down to understand it deeply from the perspectives of those most qualified to provide knowledge about it; the students involved in the experience. The broader relevance here is not about empirical generalization to other students; rather, as Mason (1996) frames it, it is about theoretical generalization or what can be generalized theoretically from a particular study. Theoretical generalization is complex and involves numerous strategies (Mason, 1996); however, for our inquiry-based study it might mean that the intricacies of group learning that are uncovered, analyzed, and theorized in this setting are potentially relevant beyond the setting. As Mason puts it, lessons learned from our "detailed and holistic explanation of one setting, or set of processes [can be used to] frame relevant questions about others" (p. 154). Further, depending on how similar other settings are to our classroom as we've defined it, we may be able to draw conclusions about other group-oriented environments as well from our deep look at learning in one classroom setting.

So What? Final Thoughts

Our SoTL study of student learning in an inquiry-based classroom can take on many forms depending on the researcher's interests, disciplinary background, training, and paradigmatic assumptions. As SoTL practitioners develop their projects, they would benefit from taking the time to reflect on and articulate a tradition of inquiry and its assumptions. (If the elements of comparison offered here don't resonate, we can bring our own disciplinary nuances to the table to extend this thinking.) This critical moment will serve them well as they collect and analyze what counts for them as data and as they share their research with colleagues.

More broadly, as we work to clarify and make visible to each other our diverse methodological underpinnings within the strategic site of SoTL, presumably we can come to understand and hence value different ways of knowing about student learning. These discussions are part of the "cross-training" Poole (2012, p. 139) talks about. If we are to move toward a "transdisciplinary" (p. 140) ideal, as Poole advises, we need to teach and learn from each other. I look forward to continuing this conversation as we share our methodological thinking in the field of SoTL.

References

Bryman, A. (2001). *Quality and quantity in social research.* New York, NY: Routledge.

Burgess, R.G. (1988). Conversations with a purpose: The ethnographic interview in educational research. *Studies in Qualitative Methodology, 1,* 137–155.

Chick, N. (2014). "Methodologically sound" under the "big tent": An ongoing conversation. *International Journal for the Scholarship of Teaching and Learning, 8*(2), Article 3.

Fox Keller, E. (1985). *Reflections on gender and science.* New Haven, CT: Yale University Press.

Hamilton, J. & Schonwetter, D.J. (2015, February). Are we asking the right questions? Setting an agenda for research in educational development. *Preconference session at the Educational Developers Caucus Conference,* Winnipeg, MB.

Harding, S. (1991). *Whose science? Whose knowledge? Thinking from women's lives.* Ithaca, NY: Cornell University Press.

Holstein, J. A., & Gubrium, J. F. (2002). Active interviewing. In D. Weinberg (Ed.), *Qualitative research methods* (pp. 112–126). Oxford, England: Blackwell.

Huber, M., & Hutchings, P. (2005). *The advancement of learning: Building the teaching commons.* San Francisco, CA: Jossey-Bass.

Hutchings, P. (2000). *Opening lines: Approaches to the scholarship of teaching and learning.* Menlo Park, CA: Carnegie Foundation for the Advancement of Teaching and Learning.

Kalin, J. (2012). Doing what comes naturally? Student perceptions and use of collaborative technologies. *International Journal for the Scholarship of Teaching and Learning, 6*(1), Article 10. doi:10.20429/ijsotl.2012.060110

Manarin, K. (2012). Reading value: Student choice in reading strategies. *Pedagogy, 12,* 281–297. https://provost.uni.edu/sites/default/files/documents/reading_value_0.pdf

Martin, E. (1992). *The woman in the body: A cultural analysis of reproduction.* Boston, MA: Beacon Press.

Mason, J. (1996). *Qualitative researching*. London, England: Sage.

Miller-Young, J. & Yeo, M. (2015). Conceptualizing and communicating SoTL: A framework for the field. *Teaching & Learning Inquiry,* 3(2), 37–53.

Poole, G. (2012). Square one: What is research? In K. McKinney (Ed.), *The scholarship of teaching and learning in and across the disciplines* (pp. 135–151). Bloomington, IN: Indiana University Press.

Potter, M. K., & Wuetherick, B. (2015). Who is represented in the teaching commons?: SoTL through the lenses of arts and humanities. *Canadian Journal for the Scholarship of Teaching and Learning,* 6(2), Article 2.

Woolf, J. (2017). An analytical autoethnographical account of using inquiry-based learning in a graduate research methods course. *Canadian Journal for the Scholarship of Teaching and Learning,* 8(1), Article 5.

6

ENSURING DESIGN ALIGNMENT IN SoTL INQUIRY

Merging Research Purpose and Methods

Robin Mueller

When the word *alignment* comes to mind, I tend to think of things like the calibration of the wheels on my vehicle, a relatively straightforward kind of alignment to achieve. However, applying the principles of alignment to the scholarship of teaching and learning (SoTL) research is a bit different, and ensuring project alignment can be a challenging process. So when we develop SoTL inquiry projects, how do we begin in a way that is likely to lead to design alignment? I have developed a framework to guide this process in a way that builds on Biggs's (1996, 2014) concept of constructive alignment, or teaching design that intentionally matches classroom activities, learning assessments, and predefined learning outcomes. I have modified and extended this idea to SoTL research, where alignment is characterized by the process of matching research methods to a clearly articulated research purpose.

Conceptualizing Alignment

Before launching our discussion about alignment, let's paint a picture of what typically happens to prompt misalignment in SoTL research. I'll use an example from my own entry to SoTL when I was interested in researching a pedagogical strategy called structured controversy as an approach to teaching difficult subject matter in an interdisciplinary leadership course. As I mulled this over, I kept coming back to the *how* or the details pertaining to how

I could investigate what I was curious about. I considered how research was typically structured in my own discipline, focusing on my own comfort level as someone who was brand new to formal inquiry. I kept returning to the method with which I was most familiar at that time and that I thought would be easiest to use. I decided to design a survey to learn more about implementing structured controversy in my classroom.

Now, let's break down this scenario and examine how it might lead to misalignment. To move this along, I use a metaphor: SoTL research as a vehicle (see Figure 6.1). Visualize a car sitting stationary on a prairie road. The car's engine can symbolize the topic or the phenomenon that a researcher is interested in knowing more about. SoTL phenomena can be concrete or conceptual in nature and are directly or indirectly linked to student learning in higher education (Felten, 2013). Like an engine, the topic (or phenomenon of interest) is what powers the research. The driver is the researcher, who controls the direction and acceleration of the vehicle and the inquiry. The body of the car is the research method, or the aspect of inquiry that enables data collection, just as the body of a vehicle provides a physical mechanism to get from one location to another. The research question is the destination, or where the vehicle is headed, and the ultimate goal is to reach the destination or to answer the question. The engine, the body of the vehicle, and the driver must all be aligned with the destination to actually get there, just as the topic, researcher, and methods must be aligned to eventually answer a research question. This metaphor helps to illustrate why misalignment occurs when

Figure 6.1. Metaphor for SoTL design alignment.

Source. Art by Daniel Fortier. Reprinted with permission.

a SoTL project is conceptualized by making methodological decisions first. The inquiry often stalls rather than moves forward because the researcher has the shell of a vehicle in place but nothing to power it and nowhere to go.

Let's return to my project, where I was using structured controversy to teach difficult subject matter. At the time I developed this study I was new to research generally and felt best equipped to design survey tools. I started with the method and built a survey with a lot of Likert-type questions and added the odd opportunity for participant comments. However, after collecting the survey data, I realized that they told me little about implementing a structured controversy and even less about the student learning outcomes that resulted. Without a clearly articulated research purpose to begin with, I wound up collecting a lot of data that were difficult to interpret and apply because they were not appropriately contextualized.

Getting Started: Articulating a Research Purpose

How do we begin, if not with method? To get started, it is essential to consider the purpose, or the concrete rationale that includes overarching aims, goals, and intentions. I have used Booth, Colomb, and Williams's (2008) research principles in combination with the idea of constructive alignment to build a model that can be used to develop a purpose in SoTL research. I want to emphasize that this is just one way of approaching the task; researchers using the practices of grounded theory, for example, engage in a completely different process. However, I have found that the model described here is useful for researchers at all stages of familiarity with SoTL and offers a straightforward approach to thinking about and developing a purpose.

According to the model I have developed, purpose in SoTL research consists of three elements: topic, questions, and the significance of the project (Figure 6.2). The components of purpose are influenced by several external factors, including the researcher's disciplinary expertise, personal experience, and the teaching and learning context of the inquiry. The elements of purpose and the external factors depicted in Figure 6.2 are best made explicit when getting started with SoTL research as they collectively form a baseline for ensuring alignment in a project. Although this doesn't have to be a linear process, it is typically most effective to make decisions about the elements of purpose by intentionally considering each element.

Leveraging Disciplinary Expertise, Experience, and Context

SoTL has been metaphorically described as a "big tent" (Huber & Hutchings, 2005, p. 30) that is meant to be interdisciplinary. Although the presence of multiple disciplinary backgrounds in SoTL increases "our confidence in

Figure 6.2. Elements of the purpose of SoTL research.

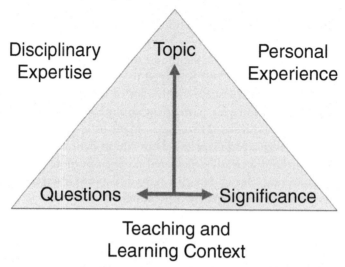

research designed to understand [the] complex world" (Poole, 2013, p. 137) of teaching and learning, it can also seem daunting for those who are new to SoTL. An effective step toward ensuring design alignment, in addition to fostering a sense of self-efficacy, is to start with one's own discipline, experience, and context, or that of the research team. This includes making an explicit note of (a) the typical purposes of research in one's home discipline, even if they are not routinely expressed; (b) the researcher's strengths, or the aspects of research that one does well and enjoys; (c) the researcher's methodological knowledge, or the research methods one knows how to use effectively; (d) the most memorable personal experiences with teaching and learning; and (e) a detailed account of the context for the SoTL research, including the class, departmental, institutional, and national dynamics. No methodological commitments are made at this point; this is not the appropriate time to start asking how to implement a study. Mapping the background and context becomes a launching point for thinking about the topics and questions in the SoTL domain that are of interest and ensures that the research purpose is intrinsically interesting and applicable.

Choosing a Topic

I rely on another metaphor when discussing the process of choosing a topic: thinking about the range of available SoTL topics as an all-you-can-eat buffet featuring every type of food imaginable. Typically, people choose from a buffet based on personal preference, dietary need, level of satiety, or desire to try something new; implicit criteria help narrow the scope of options. Choosing a topic for SoTL inquiry works in much the same way, although with different criteria. As we ponder all the options on the SoTL buffet, we may use criteria such as what is of interest to us, what is directly applicable to us, what has piqued our curiosity, or what we must investigate first to make progress with a broader research agenda. Many SoTL newcomers have a research idea in mind, so the challenge is not selecting but narrowing a topic. It's important to resist the urge to format the topic as a question at this point; although moving to a question can increase specificity, it tends to restrict creative thinking and limit the range of potential options under consideration.

We next begin the task of focusing a topic by adding specifiers: verbs, nouns, adjectives, or adverbs that provide context or imply some kind of action (Booth et al., 2008). After adding specifiers, a topic can be stated as a claim rather than a descriptor. For example, let's draw on the project about structured controversy from my earlier scenario. The following sequence demonstrates how I might move from a topic descriptor to a claim:

- Generate initial topic descriptor: using structured controversy to teach difficult subject matter
- Add specifiers: perspective taking, enables, deep, threshold concept, among, senior undergraduate students, capstone leadership course
- Frame the topic as a claim: Using structured controversy to teach students about perspective taking enables deep learning of this threshold concept among senior undergraduate students in a capstone leadership course

Stating a topic as a claim does not negate exploratory research, nor does it mean that a researcher is committed to that claim. Ultimately, the research results may support, contradict, or change the claim. This initial statement of a claim is simply a way of arriving at a level of specificity that will enable the development of a focused and well-aligned research agenda.

Asking the Best Questions

Brainstorming research questions is typically most productive when we let our preconceptions go and really engage in imaginative freewheeling. In my consultation practice, I recommend that people come up with at least 10 to 20 questions related to their chosen topic as a starting point. After generating this list of questions, it becomes easier to quickly identify important themes and connections in a topic area and to isolate the questions that most need attending to. In the end, I suggest choosing the questions that are the most interesting, most significant, or that need to be answered first. Additionally, the most powerful SoTL research questions are those that generate curiosity, reveal assumptions, and create a sense of underlying momentum. Good questions inherently make us want to answer them (Vogt, Brown, & Isaacs, 2003). Figure 6.3 provides an illustration of how research question brainstorming might look with my structured controversy example. Following this kind of exercise, my task would be to review, assess, and consolidate the brainstormed list to craft a compelling research question. An example of an appropriate question resulting from this process would be, How is structured controversy best implemented in a capstone leadership development course to enable deep learning about perspective taking?

Significance

The word *significance* is used here in a way that differs from statistical significance; rather, it implies importance. Significance is part of the research purpose because it is an essential aspect of aligning with the SoTL imperatives to (a) influence student learning (Trigwell, 2013) and (b) make research about teaching and learning "appropriately public" (Felten, 2013, p. 122). In other words, SoTL inquiry must matter to a broader community of students, scholars, and practitioners. To determine the significance of a research proposal, we can ask the following questions: Why does the research matter? Will people think it is important? To whom will it apply, and how will that audience benefit? How will the research make a difference to teaching and learning practice? How will it contribute to the broader SoTL discipline? Creating a case for significance is key to a project's purpose; it not only

Figure 6.3. Illustration of question brainstorming and identification of links.

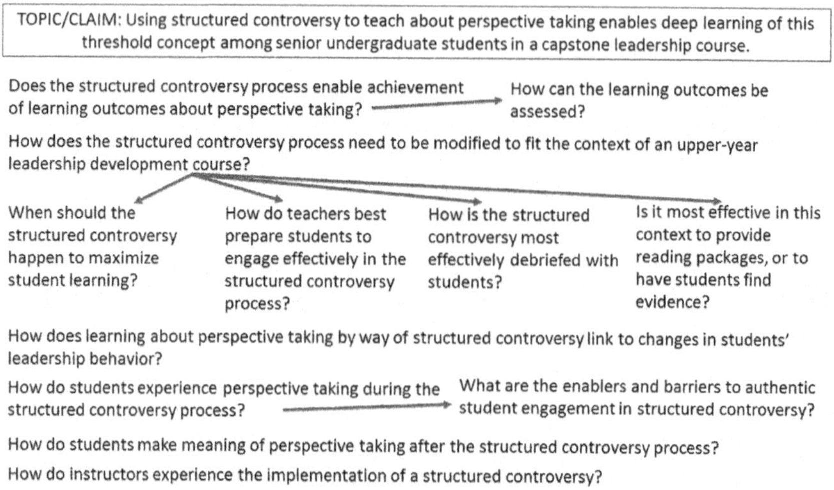

TOPIC/CLAIM: Using structured controversy to teach about perspective taking enables deep learning of this threshold concept among senior undergraduate students in a capstone leadership course.

Does the structured controversy process enable achievement of learning outcomes about perspective taking? → How can the learning outcomes be assessed?

How does the structured controversy process need to be modified to fit the context of an upper-year leadership development course?

When should the structured controversy happen to maximize student learning?

How do teachers best prepare students to engage effectively in the structured controversy process?

How is the structured controversy most effectively debriefed with students?

Is it most effective in this context to provide reading packages, or to have students find evidence?

How does learning about perspective taking by way of structured controversy link to changes in students' leadership behavior?

How do students experience perspective taking during the structured controversy process? → What are the enablers and barriers to authentic student engagement in structured controversy?

How do students make meaning of perspective taking after the structured controversy process?

How do instructors experience the implementation of a structured controversy?

establishes intrinsic motivation for completing the research but also clarifies the rationale for a project's contribution to the SoTL field. Given the topic and questions I generated as part of my example about the structured controversy project, significance becomes evident. The data collected in this project would provide evidence of the interdisciplinary potential of structured controversy and would be immediately applicable to prompt deep learning of difficult subject matter.

Matching Purpose With Method

Selecting research methods to align with a project's purpose is often viewed as the most mysterious part of creating a research agenda. There is no distinctive SoTL method and no methodological approach that is consistently advocated in the discipline. The methodological opportunities for SoTL research are endless; furthermore, the field relies on applications of multiple methods to generate meaningful representations of the complexity that characterizes teaching and learning (Poole, 2013). There are no inherently right or wrong answers when it comes to methodological choices in SoTL research, so these decisions are guided primarily by an assessment of relational fit and alignment with the research purpose. I pose the following key questions to SoTL researchers who are grappling with method:

1. What kind of data would best answer your research questions? In this context, *data* refers to "anything you find 'out there' relevant to answering your research question" (Booth et al., 2008, p. 32).
2. What methods or instruments would enable you to collect the data that would best answer your research questions?

Burns (2016) explicitly showcased research purpose and methodological alignment in the field of sustainability education. Her topic was framed as a claim: Particular pedagogical approaches can foster sustainability leadership in higher education. She also provided the reader with a strong rationale for significance, identifying a pressing need for leaders to address sustainability challenges locally and globally. She then demonstrated how the methods employed throughout the project were accordingly aligned with her purpose and were designed in an intentionally emergent manner. In her conclusion, Burns explicitly indicated how the methods used and the data collected served to answer the research questions she had formulated.

Focusing on these questions helps direct those who are new to SoTL away from methods that are most comfortable (or data that are most easily collected) and toward methods that are most appropriate given the research purpose. Evidence of good design alignment may be implicit or explicit in writing about SoTL research. Often, some aspects of the research purpose are more clearly articulated than others; readers may have to look carefully to identify all of the aspects of design alignment in a published SoTL article.

Let me tell a story about what might happen as researchers engage in this kind of well-aligned methodological consideration. I was once planning to embark on a SoTL research project that featured an exploration of values in teaching and learning. Contrary to my expectations, the process of planning my research purpose and aligning methods accordingly revealed that the best way to answer one of my questions was by way of factor analysis, a statistical manipulation of quantitative data. I am an educational researcher with a background in theater and leadership education, and over the years my methodological preferences have landed squarely within the domains of narrative inquiry and performance ethnography. I felt stuck. My options included abandoning that part of the research, learning how to do factor analysis, recruiting help from a colleague, or creating some sort of combination of these. Although I opted for a combination, the point is that researchers might not find themselves in their methodological comfort zones. Although this requires some problem-solving, it is far preferable to ending up in a quagmire of useless data because the method did not match the research purpose.

Mercer-Mapstone and Kuchel (2016) claimed that learning outcomes in science communication would be improved if teachers had access to lesson planning templates and resources. Their methods were aligned with their disciplinary expertise and their research purpose: They designed a mixed-methods approach combining surveys, interviews, and evaluations of student work to gauge student learning regarding communication outcomes and to better understand student and teacher experiences with the activity templates. They concluded by linking their methods and results to the research questions and reinforcing the significance of the study.

Why Bother With Alignment?

I first began thinking about this approach to research design alignment when providing consultation to colleagues who were proposing projects for teaching and learning grant funding. In my experience with these conversations, proactive thinking about alignment generates curiosity and encourages methodological innovation, leading to stronger research projects. Using such explicit strategies to prompt alignment is helpful for newcomers and experienced SoTL researchers alike, as the strategies generate confidence and self-efficacy by allowing researchers to quickly and efficiently focus their effort. Aligning methods with purpose enables people to determine what kinds of data are most relevant to their research and to then use optimal approaches for collecting that data. Finally, all these benefits regarding alignment also yield a framework for people to talk about their SoTL research in ways that are accessible, grounded, and well substantiated, which goes a long way to better ensuring the dissemination of our important research results in and beyond the SoTL discipline.

References

Biggs, J. (1996). Enhancing teaching through constructive alignment. *Higher Education, 32,* 347–364. Retrieved from http://edukologija.vdu.lt/en/system/files/ConstrutivismAligment_Biggs_96.pdf

Biggs, J. (2014). Constructive alignment in university teaching. *HERDSA Review of Higher Education* 1, 5–22. Retrieved from https://tru.ca/__shared/assets/herdsa33493.pdf

Booth, W. C., Colomb, G. G., & Williams, J. M. (2008). *The craft of research* (3rd ed.). Chicago, IL: University of Chicago Press.

Burns, H. L. (2016). Learning sustainability leadership: An action research study of a graduate leadership course. *International Journal for the Scholarship of Teaching and Learning, 10*(2), Article 8. doi:10.20429/ijsotl.2016.100208

Felten, P. (2013). Principles of good practice in SoTL. *Teaching & Learning Inquiry, 1*(1), 121–125. Retrieved from http://dx.doi.org/10.20343/teachlearninqu.1.1.121

Huber, M. T., & Hutchings, P. (2005). *The advancement of learning: Building the teachingcommons.* San Francisco, CA: Jossey-Bass.

Mercer-Mapstone, L. D., & Kuchel, L. J. (2016). Integrating communication skills into undergraduate science degrees: A practical and evidence based approach. *Teaching & Learning Inquiry, 4*(2). doi:10.20343/teachlearninqu.4.2.11

Poole, G. (2013). Square one: What is research? In K. McKinney (Ed.), *SoTL in & Across the Disciplines* (pp. 136–151). Bloomington, IN: Indiana University Press.

Trigwell, K. (2013). Evidence of the impact of scholarship of teaching and learning purposes. *Teaching & Learning Inquiry, 1*(1), 95–105. Retrieved from: http://tlijournal.com/tli/index.php/TLI/article/view/35/10

Vogt, E. E., Brown, J., & Isaacs, D. (2003). *The art of powerful questions: Catalyzing insight, innovation, and action.* Mill Valley, CA: Whole Systems Associates.

7

RESPECT, JUSTICE, AND DOING GOOD

The Ethics Review

Ryan C. Martin

For the past nine years I have been working with teaching and learning scholars as they navigate the complicated world of research ethics as it applies to the scholarship of teaching and learning (SoTL). I have consistently heard from researchers a litany of concerns and complaints about the ethics review process, the people involved, and even the need for ethical oversight in the first place. I understand where these concerns are coming from. The process sometimes feels overly detailed, too subjective, unnecessary, and unfriendly to SoTL. When we add that so many SoTL scholars' disciplines do not regularly interact with ethics review boards (e.g., arts, humanities), the process can feel even more daunting. That said, I argue that despite these complications, ethics review is a critical process for SoTL, and it is imperative for SoTL scholars to learn to work effectively with ethics review boards. In turn, review boards must learn to work effectively with SoTL scholars.

The Belmont Report (National Commission, 1979) should be required reading for anyone who plans on doing research with human participants. It describes the fundamental values at the core of ethical research: respect for people, beneficence, and justice.

Before I go any further, I want to take a moment to contextualize my comments. First, because I work in the United States, much of my discussion of research ethics is framed around the *Belmont Report* (National Commission for the Protection of Human Subjects of Biomedical and Behavioral Research, 1979) and the federal regulations in Protection of Human Subjects (2009). I understand that some readers work in other countries and may be unfamiliar with these documents.

However, the principles in the *Belmont Report* (National Commission, 1979) and the federal regulations (Protection of Human Subjects, 2009) are by and large consistent with those contained in other frequently used research ethics documents; I hope my comments will apply in a general sense to audiences outside the United States. Second, as a psychologist, I have been well trained to use the word *participants* rather than *subjects* when referring to human beings in research. However, because I'm writing for nonpsychologists and because the federal regulations use the word *subjects*, I use this term throughout this chapter.

Reflections of a SoTL Ethics Geek

I start with a few important reflections regarding institutional review boards (IRBs) and SoTL. First, IRBs were not in any way designed with SoTL in mind. They were constructed, for the most part, for biomedical research (Bankert & Amdur, 2006). Thus, the policies in place often feel overly onerous or irrelevant to those of us trying to study teaching and learning (Why, no, I wasn't planning on drawing blood from my students.). Second, in many situations IRBs have treated SoTL scholars with disdain or even hostility. I am frequently contacted by scholars from across the country who are attempting to conduct research on their teaching and tell me about the difficulty they have had with their IRBs. In many, if not most, of those cases, their concerns were warranted. The IRBs in question were behaving in a way that was inconsistent with the federal regulations. Third, unique ethical concerns exist in SoTL, and we need to be aware of them. Too often I hear SoTL scholars say, "Why do we even have to do this?" or "There are no risks in this research." Such claims are simply untrue. Like all research, there are risks to subjects, and we need to be aware of them. Fourth, SoTL scholars, like all researchers, have rights in the IRB process. IRBs are not all-knowing masters of all things related to research ethics. They make mistakes and sometimes embrace flawed ideas and unfair policies. SoTL scholars have the right to respond to such policies, and IRBs should be forced to operate in accordance with the federal regulations for the Protection of Human Subjects (2009).

Why Must I Do This?

One of the first questions I am often asked by those new to the IRB process is, Why must I do this? Although I understand why people ask the question,

On the surface, SoTL seems relatively benign from an ethical perspective, especially when compared to other more obviously invasive forms of research like biomedical or psychological research. Stockley and Balkwill (2013) nicely provided the reasons it is so important for SoTL scholars to pay attention to research ethics.

the answers are relatively simple. We must do this because (a) we are doing research, and (b) research is rarely, if ever, benign. All research has potential risks. Although a SoTL study may not be the same as biomedical research on the side effects of a new drug or as research on the outcome of an experimental surgery, there are still risks we must consider, specifically related to coercion and the potentially deeply personal nature of the data we so obtain.

The first issue, coercion, is of particular concern with SoTL because of the nature of the relationships we often have with our subjects (Martin, 2014). Specifically, because our subjects are typically students enrolled in our classes, they may feel compelled to participate because there is a direct benefit to participation (e.g., course credit, extra credit) or because they want to gain our approval. They may, in fact, feel that refusing to participate would lead to a lower grade in the course. Perhaps they feel compelled to participate because they are planning on asking us to serve as a reference for them in the future. Regardless of the reason, the dual relationship as student and subject may lead to a diminished ability to make an autonomous decision about participation in the study. The capacity for subjects to make such independent and autonomous decisions to participate in research is a cornerstone of research ethics, referred to as "Respect for Persons" (National Commission, 1979, p. 2), and we simply must go above and beyond to protect the rights of our students to freely decide if they want to be research subjects.

The second ethical issue we often run into with SoTL concerns the nature of the data we collect. As teachers, we often have access to very personal information that students provide as part of class activities. In an

Swenson and McKarthy (2012) offered a nice description of the steps to take when doing SoTL and how those steps should be driven by federal regulations.

English course, for example, students may have written deeply personal memoirs that an instructor could use as data. In one of my larger courses on mental illness, I have students write journal entries on what they are learning and how they feel about the content. Students often reveal very personal information about their own mental health history or the mental health history of their loved ones. This could technically be considered data and, in fact, as part of the federal regulations for the Protection of Human Subjects (2009), might even be available for use without obtaining consent under exemption No. 4, "research involving the collection or study of existing data" (46.101.b). To use such personal information without the consent of students, even if it meets federal regulations, is ethically dubious. When students write such things as part of a course, they assume the material will remain private.

Fine, I'll Do It. Where Do I Start?

The natural follow-up from someone who now understands why ethics approval is so important is feeling lost about how to proceed. Thus, the question I often hear next is, Where do I start? The first thing I tell researchers is to consult their institution's IRB website for policies and procedure well in advance of the research. Most IRB websites have a fairly clear explanation of submission procedures and policies, along with specific forms that need to be completed. Some of the better IRB websites have instructions for first-time submitters, and some may even have guidelines for submissions related to SoTL, although this is rare. If the policies and procedures are unclear, the chair of the IRB should be able to answer any questions new submitters may have.

Second, I advise SoTL scholars who are new to ethics review to consider their institution's center for instructional or professional development as a useful resource. Staff at such centers are typically very familiar with the ethics related to SoTL and have worked with their institutions' ethics boards. They likely have a feel for the procedures, relevant polices, and even the personalities involved. Contacting that center for guidance and resources might be a useful way to get through the process smoothly.

Okay, I Submitted, and My Research Was Not Approved

It's rare, but I sometimes consult with SoTL scholars whose research is denied. When that happens I make several suggestions. First, I tell them to read through the feedback from the IRB, if provided, to see what the problem is. It might be because of mistakes in the way the IRB interpreted their procedures, or the IRB's concerns with the research may be easily fixed. Second, if the problems with the research are unclear, I tell them to contact the chair of the IRB to get a list of the specific concerns. In that conversation, they need to ask for details; make sure they have a clear sense of what the problems are; and, most important, understand how those problems increase risk to subjects. In other words, the IRB's job is to ensure that the researchers take steps to minimize the risk to subjects of participation in the study. Every concern the board brings up should be tied, somehow, to risk. This means that the IRB should not be criticizing things like methodology, writing, or the research's value.

After consulting with the IRB about the reasons the research was denied, researchers will usually have some sort of plan for addressing the concerns and moving forward. If they still do not have a resolution, there are a few more steps I encourage them to take. First, I tell them that the IRB chairperson cannot deny their research on his or her own. The chairperson can refuse to approve it but then needs to consult with the rest of the IRB members, who then vote on the submission. Second, if researchers feel they are being treated unfairly or that the IRB is in the wrong, I encourage them to contact the person or group the IRB reports to at the institution to try to resolve the situation. Before doing so, however, they should consult the federal regulations and other IRB experts to make sure they have a clear understanding of the expectations and to make sure their position is supported.

This All Sounds Like a Lot of Extra Work

I was speaking at a conference a few years ago on the very topic mentioned in the heading, and when I was finished someone asked, "What if I don't care about publishing? What if I just want to know if my approach worked? Can't I just skip the IRB process and collect and analyze the data for myself?" What was interesting about this is that when he asked the question, about a third of the room started nodding along with him in agreement. To me, the question really reflected how a lot of teachers feel about IRBs and SoTL.

The short answer to his question is very simple. Yes, teachers can skip the IRB if they don't want to publish their results. The IRB is only responsible for evaluating *research*, which is defined as "a systematic investigation, including research development, testing and evaluation, designed to develop or contribute to generalizable knowledge" (Protection of Human Subjects, 2009, 46.102.d). If teachers are not planning on trying to contribute to generalizable knowledge (i.e., publish or present), it's not research. They still have teaching ethics they should follow, but the IRB is no longer relevant when we aren't talking about research.

The longer answer to his question is that it would be a shame not to publish interesting findings because of fear or frustration with the IRB process. Like anything we do, the more often we work through the IRB process, the easier it gets. It is understandably daunting at first, but once teachers learn the procedures, forms, and expectations, it becomes more systematic. Similarly, we can build the IRB process into our research process in such a way that it ends up being very little extra work. For example, I do not bother working through any of the logistics of my research until I start working on the IRB proposal. I figure out all the details of my data collection while putting the proposal together so that it ends up being a natural part of my research process rather than an extra step.

More important, though, is that when SoTL scholars decide not to publish interesting and important findings, they withhold potential contributions from other teachers and future students. Remember the three principles discussed in the *Belmont Report* (National Commission, 1979): respect for people, beneficence, and justice. I mentioned respect for people earlier as a place where SoTL sometimes suffers because of the possibility for coercion. These other two principles, though, justice and beneficence, are where SoTL often shines. In the case of justice, the work of SoTL scholars typically benefits the very population we research. Unlike other research, in which one population may be the subject of research but the benefits of the research go to a different population, students are the ones who bear the burdens and benefits of SoTL. This is a strength of what we do. Similarly, with beneficence, we see that the *Belmont Report* makes a strong statement that we should not merely avoid harm when doing research; rather, we should work to maximize possible benefits. In fact, the report states unequivocally that efforts to secure our subjects' well-being are "an obligation" (National Commission, 1979, p. 3) of researchers.

I argue that by not publishing our findings, we miss out on an opportunity to do the most possible good and provide the most possible justice. If we run our students through a data collection process or some other tedious intervention, and we find that what we did worked and they learned, we should feel some obligation to share the findings with other teachers so that our subjects' work was not in vain and so future students will also see the benefits.

References

Bankert, E. A., & R. J. Amdur. (2006). *Institutional review board: Management and function*. Sudbury, MA: Jones & Bartlett.

Martin, R. C. (2014). The ethics of SoTL. In R. A. R. Gurung & J. H. Wilson (Eds.), *Doing the scholarship of teaching and learning: Measuring systematic changes to teaching and improvements in learning* (pp. 59–72). San Francisco, CA: Jossey-Bass.

National Commission for the Protection of Human Subjects of Biomedical and Behavioral Research. (1979). *The Belmont report: Ethical principles and guidelines for the protection of human subjects of research.* Washington DC: U.S. Government Printing Office.

Protection of Human Subjects, 45 C.F.R. 46 (2009).

Stockley, D., & Balkwill, L. (2013). Raising awareness of research ethics in SoTL: The role of educational developers. *Canadian Journal for the Scholarship of Teaching and Learning, 4,* 1–8.

Swenson, E. V., & McCarthy, A. (2012). Ethically conducting the scholarship of teaching and learning research. In E. R. Landrum, & M. A. McCarthy (Eds.), *Teaching ethically: Challenges and opportunities* (pp. 21–29). Washington DC: American Psychological Association.

PART TWO

METHODS AND METHODOLOGIES

8

METHODS AND
MEASURES MATTER

Meaningful Questionnaires

Trent W. Maurer

When I consult with scholars new to the scholarship of teaching and learning (SoTL)—and often with those not new to SoTL—I typically start by telling them about one of my greatest frustrations as a reviewer for SoTL conferences and publications: More often than not, the methods and measures scholars use do not generate information that actually answers the SoTL question they have asked. This is frustrating for two reasons. First, as SoTL scholar, I am frustrated because that's poor scholarly practice (Glassick, Huber, & Maeroff, 1997) and generates poor quality scholarship. Such scholarship is unlikely to make any meaningful contribution to the SoTL literature and reflects poorly on SoTL as an area of legitimate scholarly inquiry. Second, as a teacher, I am frustrated because it means the scholars can't answer the important teaching and learning question driving their investigation, which means it is not likely to generate any meaningful insight into understanding or improving teaching and learning. At its most basic, this problem represents wasted effort and lost opportunities.

The question for SoTL scholars then becomes how to best align their methods and measures with their SoTL questions (see chapter 6 for excellent advice on this alignment). Even if I craft the most amazingly meaningful SoTL question, if I don't carefully select appropriate methods and measures to answer that question, then the data I collect will at best be of limited value and at worst will mislead me about what's really going on. It could even damage the teaching and learning process under investigation.

Before diving any deeper into this topic, a critical explanation of terminology is necessary. The words *survey* and *questionnaire* are often used interchangeably by those without specific training or expertise in survey methods; this is a fundamental misconception that actually reveals an underlying bias toward questionnaires among those conflating the terms. The word *survey* refers to the overarching method for collecting data or information. The word *questionnaire* refers to one type of measure that can be used with survey methods in which the measure is self-administered by the participants (i.e., the participants read though the questionnaire and answer the questions at their own pace). The other type of measure that can be used with survey methods is interviews in which the measure is administered by an interviewer (i.e., the interviewer asks the questions). Both types of measures can include open-ended questions (e.g., What was one thing that helped you to learn the material in this course?), closed-ended questions (e.g., Using the following scale, how much did the instructor's explanations help you learn the material in this course? Not at all, a small amount, a moderate amount, a large amount?), or both. Questionnaires can be administered individually, for example, having a participant come to a designated testing room and fill out the questionnaire; in group settings, such as passing out a questionnaire to a class and having each student fill it out; by mail, having participants complete a questionnaire on their own time and mail it back to you; or on the Internet, directing participants to an Internet link and having them complete the questionnaire found there. Interviews can be administered face-to-face, by telephone, or through video chatting software. The advantage of interviews is that the interviewer can ask participants for clarification on their responses or follow-up questions; the disadvantages are the greater time, expense, and expertise in interviewing skills required to do this successfully (Johnson & Morgan, 2016). These disadvantages are why many who use survey methods rely primarily or exclusively on questionnaires, an overreliance that explains why many conflate the terms *survey* and *questionnaire*. Questionnaires are often they only type of surveys they see.

Because so many who use survey methods rely on questionnaires, I focus most of my discussion there, but I want to stress that often interviews are actually the more appropriate choice (see chapter 10 for a detailed explanation of how to conduct interviews in SoTL). For example, if I'm investigating a teaching and learning phenomenon that hasn't been explored in the literature, or even one that has been explored but not yet in my discipline or context, starting with open-ended interview questions and asking follow-up or clarification questions would be the best way to go (Boynton & Greenhalgh, 2004; Howitt & Cramer, 2000). Without the ability to probe participants for further explanation or clarification, it's possible that I could misunderstand their responses or miss important insights about the underlying issues. All too often, I see SoTL scholars skip this step and jump right to the closed-ended questionnaires they have created, which rarely results in meaningful insight. I recommend taking the time to figure out what they should be asking before they put together a questionnaire.

I also have to acknowledge that the sheer scope of issues involved in survey methods means that detailed recommendations and techniques for questionnaire construction, reliability and validity analyses, and so forth are beyond what can be addressed in a single chapter. One of the best pieces of advice I can give SoTL scholars who are considering using surveys in their work is that if they do not have extensive training or expertise in survey methods, they should consult with someone who does when they are designing their investigation. Fortunately, many established SoTL scholars are highly collaborative and highly generative, so finding this kind of mentoring is not as difficult as it might seem. In a pinch, if it's not possible to consult with an expert, I recommend at least reading several texts that provide an overview of the issues involved (DeVellis, 2016; Fowler, 2013; Johnson & Morgan, 2016; McCoach, Gable, & Madura, 2013).

With those caveats acknowledged, I'd like to talk a little bit about how I approach using surveys in my SoTL work, with particular attention to the questions I ask that help guide my decisions. Throughout this process, I ask myself the same question over and over again: How do these measures relate to my guiding questions, and will they provide data that will help answer that question? Once I have decided on the primary question or questions I want to explore, I ask where those questions fall in Hutchings' (2000) typology of SoTL questions. For example, if I'm exploring a What is? question, then my goals are descriptive, whereas if I'm exploring a What works? question, my goals are more evaluative. For a What is? question, I'm more likely to focus on open-ended questions in my survey, and I'm more likely to try to use interviews. This allows me to collect the kind of rich, descriptive data necessary to answer a What is? kind of question.

In contrast, for a What works? question, I'm more likely to focus on direct measures of learning, especially those that allow me to explicitly compare student knowledge, performance, or skills at two or more points in time, preferably in comparison to one or more additional groups of students who were exposed to alternative teaching and learning environments. This need not require closed-ended items on a questionnaire or quantitative analyses, although typically I do use both for such questions. As pointed out in chapter 4, educational research is broader than just quantitative approaches, and SoTL could benefit from more widespread use of more qualitative approaches.

Open-ended questions can also have great value for What works? questions and are all too often overlooked as a possible option. What works?

questions implicitly ask, What doesn't work? and Why do some things work and others don't? Those types of questions are inherently open-ended, especially in new areas of SoTL research and are often ideally suited to interviews. Additionally, open-ended questions sometimes result in richer information about how students' thinking has changed. Chapter 2 provides an excellent example of how to assess students' learning by using their responses to a pre-course assignment of open-ended questions as a baseline for describing their initial thinking and measuring future changes in how the students understood and thought about a complex phenomenon.

It is also important to remember that when comparing multiple teaching methods in a What works? question, one possible outcome is that different methods may turn out to be equally effective in promoting student learning. Rather than interpreting such a result as a failure to find a better method, asking why the different methods might appear equally effective and if they are effective for different reasons could yield meaningful insight into the teaching and learning process. Open-ended questions would be necessary for this.

In such cases even measures of student satisfaction and perceptions of learning (whether closed-ended or open-ended) could have some value. Typically, such measures are given less weight in the SoTL literature because they are at best indirect measures of learning. Insofar as those measures reflect students' perspectives and voices, they do have value, but they typically tell us precious little about students' actual learning. However, such measures can have significant value when those data are triangulated with direct measures of student learning. Some of my own work has shown that sometimes students misperceive a more novel or engaging method of instruction as resulting in more learning than an alternative method, when in reality the two methods are equally effective.

After determining where my SoTL questions fall on Hutchings's (2000) typology and how that will guide my approach to the kind of information I want to collect, the next questions I typically ask concern big-picture conceptual issues in teaching and learning as they apply to my specific SoTL questions. For example, if I am interested in comparing two or more different teaching techniques to determine their influence on student learning, I have to decide if I am going to conceptualize student learning as proficiency (i.e., what students can demonstrate they know or can perform), growth (i.e., how much students have improved over time in what they can demonstrate they know or can perform), or both. There are profound implications for this choice. In higher education, most of our assessments of student learning are proficiency based; students typically receive grades based on their demonstrated level of mastery of the course material. In some

Sturges, Maurer, and Cole's (2009) study is a rare example of a SoTL project that assessed direct measures of student learning in the form of 3 tests and student perceptions of learning, engagement, and satisfaction with 11, 7, and 7 closed-ended items, respectively. By assessing both, it was possible to compare the data, and those comparisons provided an excellent example of the value that student perceptions can have if they are triangulated with direct measures of learning. The results revealed that two methods for teaching protein synthesis appeared to be equally effective in promoting student learning, as assessed by direct measures. However, students demonstrated a clear preference for the nonlecture method, reporting higher levels of satisfaction, engagement, and learning. In other words, students who were taught with the nonlecture method mistakenly thought they had learned more than students who were taught with the lecture method. These results identified a potential risk in using more engaging teaching methods, which would not have been identified without assessing both direct measures of learning and student perceptions. This study also provided a comparison of the results using a growth and a proficiency approach to learning.

situations, this is excellent practice as it mirrors the way most professional licensing and certification examinations work (e.g., to become certified, the candidate must earn a score of 70% or higher on the exam). However, proficiency-based assessments only measure mastery, and the term *learning* implies the acquisition of knowledge, skills, and so on, which also implies growth (i.e., change over time). Measuring growth requires assessment at multiple points in time, whether quantitative, qualitative, or both. If I am interested in measuring growth, it will require greater time and expense, as well as the ability to track students over time to link their responses from multiple data collection points. Sometimes practical limitations prevent using a growth conceptualization, even when it might be the most appropriate choice.

When I have answered the big-picture conceptual issue questions, I next turn to some of the nitty-gritty details that are connected to the specifics of data collection and analyses. For example, if I am planning on using a questionnaire, I search the existing SoTL literature, interdisciplinary and in multiple disciplines, to see if I can find an existing questionnaire that has previously been used (see chapter 3 for advice on searching the literature).

Even if I can't find an exact match, I may be able to find something close enough that could be adapted. As a tip from a veteran, there may be an updated version of the questionnaire. I look for works that have cited the

---

Maurer and Kropp (2015) reported on a study that used a preexisting questionnaire with 19 closed-ended items in the form of an institution-mandated student evaluation of teaching form. It was an example of a case where practical limitations (i.e., institutional policy) prevented replacing or altering the questionnaire in any way, and the study questions had to conform to the measure rather than the other way around. Because the student evaluation of teaching form was anonymous and did not collect any demographic data, it was not possible to either demographically describe the sample or link individual students' evaluations to their objective measures of learning. Their article is not an example of best practices in survey methods but rather an example of how to make the best out of a situation where such limitations are externally imposed. By using a common institutionally mandated questionnaire across multiple courses, instructors, and experimental conditions, it was possible nonetheless to draw informed conclusions about the impact of specific summative assessment strategies on student evaluations of teaching.

---

source I found and if they use a different version of the questionnaire. I also check the web page of the primary author of the questionnaire if possible for any updated information. I have even been surprised how often a quick Google search has found an updated version of a questionnaire. Additionally, when contacting the primary author of the questionnaire to ask for permission to use it, I ask if there's an updated version or a new questionnaire. If I can't find an existing questionnaire that would be appropriate to use or adapt, that means I have to develop my own (more on that later).

At this step in the process I also ask questions about statistical issues and considerations for quantitative data if I am using a closed-ended questionnaire. The scope of these questions are beyond what can be addressed in detail here but include things like identifying which statistical tests can be used for the number of independent and dependent variables, the level of measurement in the questionnaire (e.g., nominal, ordinal, ratio, or interval), and sample size. For example, how large a sample size would I need to achieve the requisite level of statistical power necessary to detect an effect of a specified size (Cohen, 1988)? Will I have a large enough sample with a single section of the course, or will I need to collect data from multiple sections of the course? If I am testing multiple different teaching techniques, can I test them in the same section of the course, or would I need multiple sections of the course? Although these are not questions about the questionnaire per se,

Reinke, Muraco, and Maurer (2016) described a disciplinary cross-institutional replication using an online questionnaire adapted from prior seminal questionnaires. The questionnaire included closed-ended and open-ended items that were clearly selected to answer the primary questions of the project and enable comparisons to previously published studies using similar questionnaires. The methods section provided an unusually detailed explanation of how the questionnaire was organized and presented to participants, and the full questionnaire was included as an appendix. The questionnaire demonstrated many best practices in questionnaire design (e.g., listing the demographic block last on the questionnaire, avoiding double-barreled questions, not assigning numbers to labeled response options, etc.). The results did not overinterpret the data and were limited to describing the quantitative and qualitative responses as well as integrating the quantitative and qualitative responses to provide a fuller picture of the state of SoTL in the discipline.

they are critical to ensuring that I collect enough and the right kind of data from the questionnaires to be able to answer the project questions.

The next step in the process is the most difficult: adapting or creating the questions or items themselves. Rarely will I be able to reuse an existing questionnaire without modifications, even if I am reusing a questionnaire I created myself. On the easier end of the continuum are questionnaires that require only minor alterations or additions (e.g., changing the frame of reference for the questions from Class X to Class Y or adding a demographic question about which class participants are enrolled in). Creating a new questionnaire entirely from scratch is on the more difficult end of the continuum. Wherever the task falls on that continuum, I ask myself the same questions: What do I want an answer to this question to tell me? What would each of the response options tell me about this question and the topic of investigation? To what extent are the wording of this question and its response options consistent with best practices in questionnaire design and scale development? How will I know if this question and its response options are being interpreted correctly by the participants? Obviously, the design of the questionnaire should be heavily influenced by the guiding questions of the project and the relevant literature. Again, I advise SoTL scholars using surveys that unless they have extensive training or expertise in survey methods, they should consult with someone who does or at least consult several texts.

When I have finished the draft of the questionnaire, the following critical steps remain before I'm ready to finalize it: (a) expert validation, (b) response process validation, and (c) pilot testing (Artino, La Rochelle, Dezee, & Gehlbach, 2014). Again, the sheer extent of each of these means that detailed explanations and recommendations are beyond the scope of what can be addressed here, and I encourage SoTL scholars to consult relevant texts. The explanations presented here are brief. Expert validation involves having experts in the content or method review the questionnaire and provide feedback on its appropriateness. This includes SoTL scholars with expertise in the topic under investigation as well as survey methodologists. It can be helpful to think of this step as a form of pre–peer review. After incorporating changes from this stage, the new draft questionnaire is ready for the next step.

Response process validation is all about finding out to what extent potential participants in the research interpret the questions and response options the way the researcher intended. For SoTL projects that have students as the participants, this step can represent a wonderful opportunity to engage in meaningful partnerships with students (e.g., Cook-Sather, Bovill, & Felten, 2014; Werder & Otis, 2010; see also chapter 5) because it requires explicitly working with students to get their perspectives on the questionnaire. There are multiple methods for conducting response process validation (Artino et al., 2014), but all of them involve querying a small group of potential participants about how they interpret the questionnaire. Feedback from this stage should be used to make further revisions to the questionnaire before pilot testing. If there are large discrepancies between how the potential participants interpreted the questionnaire and its intended meaning, it may be necessary to start over or conduct a preliminary interview survey primarily composed of open-ended questions to get a better understanding of the underlying issues.

Pilot testing is conducted to obtain initial information on the reliability and validity of the questionnaire (e.g., reliability analysis, factor analysis, and similar considerations, primarily for closed-ended questions). Briefly, reliability concerns the consistency of scores on the measure, whereas validity concerns the extent to which the measure is a sound indicator of what it is supposed to measure. The questionnaire is administered to potential participants (the exact number of which depends on multiple factors), and the resulting data are analyzed to determine if the questionnaire is sufficiently reliable and valid for use. If there are any red flags in the reliability and validity analyses (e.g., low internal consistency, an uninterpretable factor structure), revisions to the questionnaire or even starting over entirely may be necessary. Additionally, pilot testing can provide an opportunity to debug the questionnaire and data collection and entry process before proceeding with the full-scale project. I once discovered during a pilot test that the new software I had obtained to more quickly read and enter my questionnaire data couldn't actually read the data from my questionnaires at all. It turned out the software was extremely sensitive to even the smallest mistakes in formatting, and I had slightly misaligned a column, which was not visually detectable, and rendered all my questionnaires unreadable. If I hadn't realized and fixed the error before I began my main project, I would have had to enter all the responses by hand. At the end of pilot testing, and after any remaining revisions to the questionnaire are made, it is time to administer the question-naire to the intended sample of participants.

Of course just because I have finalized the questionnaire doesn't mean I am actually finished with this process. When all the data have been col-lected and analyzed, I still may not be able to answer the questions driving the project. Additional research, likely with revised or new questionnaires or interview surveys, may yet be required. However, subsequent projects can build on prior ones, including what was learned from previous surveys and from their creation, so it's helpful to view this as an iterative process, much like teaching and scholarship.

Although I believe surveys done well can help answer important ques-tions in teaching and learning and make meaningful contributions to the SoTL literature, I always caution SoTL scholars against overreliance on them, and especially on closed-ended questionnaires. First, such overreli-ance can lead to an excessive focus on quantitative approaches and positiv-ist epistemologies, denigrating or ignoring the contributions of qualitative approaches and other ways of knowing, especially in disciplines other than the natural and social sciences. There are many ways to do SoTL under the big tent (Huber & Hutchings, 2005), and we should recognize that no single way can answer all the questions (Miller-Young & Yeo, 2015; chapter 5). Second, it's easy to confuse statistical significance with practical significance, and sometimes scholars mistakenly assume that any statistically significant result is meaningful. A statistically significant result means only that there is a high degree of confidence that the statistic is reliable (typically set at a 95% confidence level in the educational and social sciences); it does not neces-sarily mean that the result is either large or meaningful. In fact, as Hattie's (2009) meta-analyses revealed, nearly every educational technique works in the sense that it has a statistically significant effect on student learning in the direction predicted. The question is not Does it work? which is a statistical significance question, but rather, How much of a difference does it make? which is an effect size question. Closer attention to effect sizes and whether they exceed Hattie's (2009) proposed threshold of Cohen's (1988) $d = 0.4$

would be more appropriate than simply focusing on statistical significance. But that is another topic, for another time.

References

Artino, A. R., Jr., La Rochelle, J. S., Dezee, K. J., & Gehlbach, H. (2014). Developing questionnaires for educational research: AMEE Guide No. 87. *Medical Teacher, 36*, 463–474. doi:10.3109/0142159X.2014.889814

Boynton, P. M., & Greenhalgh, T. (2004). Hands-on guide to questionnaire research: Selecting, designing, and developing your questionnaire. *British Medical Journal, 328*, 1312–1315. doi:10.1136/bmj.328.7451.1312

Cohen, J. (1988). *Statistical power analysis for the behavioral sciences* (2nd ed.). Hillsdale, NJ: Erlbaum.

Cook-Sather, A., Bovill, C., & Felten, P. (2014). *Engaging students as partners in learning and teaching: A guide for faculty.* San Francisco, CA: Jossey-Bass.

DeVellis, R. F. (2016). *Scale development: Theory and applications* (4th ed.). Newbury Park, CA: Sage.

Fowler, F. J. (2013). *Survey research methods* (5th ed.). Thousand Oaks, CA: Sage.

Glassick, C. E., Huber, M. T., & Maeroff, G. I. (1997). *Scholarship assessed: Evaluation of the professoriate.* San Francisco, CA: Jossey-Bass.

Hattie, J. (2009). *Visible learning: A synthesis of over 800 meta-analyses relating to achievement.* New York, NY: Routledge.

Howitt, D., & Cramer, D. (2000). *First steps in research and statistics.* London, England: Routledge.

Huber, M. T., & Hutchings, P. (2005). *The advancement of learning: Building the teaching commons.* San Francisco, CA: Jossey-Bass.

Hutchings, P. (2000). *Opening lines: Approaches to the scholarship of teaching and learning.* Menlo Park, CA: Carnegie Foundation for the Advancement of Teaching and Learning.

Johnson, R. L., & Morgan, G. B. (2016). *Survey scales: A guide to development, analysis, and reporting.* New York, NY: Guilford Press.

Maurer, T. W., & Kropp, J. (2015). The impact of the Immediate Feedback Assessment Technique on course evaluations. *Teaching & Learning Inquiry, 3*, 31–46. doi:10.20343/teachlearninqu.3.1.31

McCoach, D. B., Gable, R. K., & Madura, J. P. (2013). *Instrument development in the affective domain: School and corporate applications* (3rd ed.). New York, NY: Springer.

Miller-Young, J., & Yeo, M. (2015). Conceptualizing and communicating SoTL: A framework for the field. *Teaching and Learning Inquiry, 3*(2), 37–53. doi:10.20343/teachlearninqu.3.2.37

Reinke, J., Muraco, J., & Maurer, T. W. (2016). The state of the scholarship of teaching and learning in family science. *Family Science Review, 21*(2), 18–53.

Retrieved from http://www.familyscienceassociation.org/familysciencereview/vol21/issue2%20

Sturges, D., Maurer, T. W., & Cole, O. (2009). Understanding protein synthesis: A role-play approach in large undergraduate human anatomy and physiology courses. *Advances in Physiology Education, 33*, 103–110. doi:10.1152/advan.00004.2009

Werder, C., & Otis, M. M. (Eds.) (2010). *Engaging student voices in the study of teaching and learning*. Sterling, VA: Stylus.

9

CLASSROOM OBSERVATIONS

Exploring How Learning Works

Bill Cerbin

You can observe a lot by just watching. (Yogi Berra)

The central business of teaching is about creating changes in the minds of students—in what students know and believe and how they think. The ability to create change means that, in some way, teachers need to be constantly reading the minds of students. Are their minds focused? What are they understanding, or not understanding? What do they really think? (Nuthall, 2007, p. 23)

For those new to the scholarship of teaching and learning (SoTL), the idea of classroom observation as a method of inquiry may be unfamiliar, but observing students in our classes is probably a daily occurrence, if not an ongoing part of teaching. We notice how students respond to our explanations of a topic; how they react to questions; what they do as they work in small groups; and how they handle laboratory equipment, a paintbrush, or a spreadsheet. We use these observations to interpret student behavior and adjust our teaching. For example, students' questions and comments about a topic I am teaching reveal they are interpreting it much differently from what I intended. I can then stop to try to locate where they and I went wrong.

Nuthall's (2007) short book summarizes 40 years of research on the classroom experiences of teachers and students based on meticulous recording, observation, and interviews. It documents one surprising insight after another about student learning.

Some teachers take observation a step further and use formative assessment techniques such as clicker questions, think-pair-share, or minute papers to spot check students' thinking during class. These strategies provide a glimpse of how students interpret and make sense of the subject under discussion.

Even if we use formative assessment, it is difficult to teach and observe a class simultaneously. As one teacher put it, a class period "is like a swiftly flowing river; when you're teaching you must make judgments instantly" (Lewis, 2002, p. 38). We simply cannot attend to multiple students and events at the same time. During on-the-fly observations, we may not see the antecedents of students' responses or understand their comments, and we don't have time to ponder their meanings and implications.

A Method of Inquiry

As a method of inquiry, classroom observation involves more intentional and systematic ways to gather evidence about student learning, thinking, and behavior. In SoTL, observation is intentional in that it focuses on and is guided by research questions. I may want to know why students have difficulty understanding an important course concept, so I observe how they explain the concept or use it to solve a problem. I may want to know how students' misconceptions interfere with learning a certain theoretical perspective, so I focus on the kinds of misunderstandings that appear in their discussion and explanations of the theory. I may want to know what kinds of interactions in small groups support or impede students' learning, so I look for instances of productive and counterproductive interactions as students work in small groups. Observation is systematic in the sense that researchers decide in advance whom to observe, what to observe, and how to observe.

Classroom observation focuses on the process of learning in situ as it takes place. This is especially important if I want to explore how and why students learn or don't learn. Classroom observations produce information about

- how students respond to instruction, the interaction between teaching and learning, and how teaching affects student learning and thinking, and
- how students learn subject matter, skills, values, sensibilities, "how they interpret and construe the material, where they stumble and succeed, what confuses them, how misconceptions develop, how they put ideas together, gaps in their thinking" (Cerbin, 2011, p. 69).

"How to Study a Lesson" in Cerbin (2011) describes how to use observation in combination with other methods to study teaching and learning in a single class lesson.

Observing Learning

Observation is essential if we want to explore how learning works. Much SoTL research focuses on whether teaching strategies work and uses student performance on tests, assignments, or some other measure of learning. Much less research explores the nature of learning itself. When learning is the object of study, we explore the conditions that influence learning, especially questions about what makes learning hard. For example, instead of simply measuring how much students learn from a new strategy, we focus on how students respond to it, how it helps them overcome well-known trouble spots or misconceptions (Cerbin, 2013).

Teachers' questions about student learning are fertile grounds for observational studies. For example, in most college courses, concepts, theories, ideas, or skills pose significant challenges for students. As Perkins (2007) said, "One of the most important questions an educator can ask falls into just four words: What makes this hard?" (p. 31). Observational research can help teachers understand why students have difficulty with specific ideas or skills, an important precursor for designing instruction that advances student learning.

Classroom Observation in Action

A classroom problem that has long troubled me is the relatively low quality of work students produce in group learning tasks in my classes. I have tried a number of group learning strategies, but they don't seem to make much difference. Rather than continuing to try out different remedies, I want to see what students actually do when they work on group learning tasks in class, which is an exploratory study. I am not starting with an hypothesis; instead I want to understand what group learning looks like in my class. My reasoning is that if I understand how students are thinking and what they are doing, I might be able to identify specific weaknesses and problems, and then change instruction accordingly. I go through the following steps in planning an exploratory study to understand how learning is working, or in this case, not working, when my students work in groups.

Scope of the Study

The study will take place in one of my classes, and I plan to recruit four colleagues to participate as observers. I don't have the time to observe all my classes or observe several different types of group learning tasks.

Choosing the Task

For this observation, the task should be one that is challenging and generates a range of student performance that allows observers to examine strong as well as weak student performance. The task should make student thinking visible as much as possible, which means it is open to observation and analysis. In addition, written work serves as additional evidence about their learning and thinking. Students write answers to several prompts during the class period and produce a group summary of their work at the end.

Choosing an Observation Strategy

Interactive groups can be difficult to observe. One option is to take field notes to try to keep a running record of group members' interactions. Field notes work well when the interactions are between two people such as student to student or student to teacher. But in observing a group of more than two people, it is difficult to record each interaction and keep track of who is speaking to whom. I prefer to use observation protocols that focus on certain aspects of student thinking and behavior. When I do classroom research, I want to focus on evidence related to the purpose and goals of the study. In this study, I want to explore group learning broadly, cast a wide net, and not focus too narrowly on one type of behavior. In addition, I am curious about how groups support or impede learning and would like a close-up view of students' interactions.

It may be possible to accomplish both aims by using two different observational strategies. The first strategy I've used in lesson study research is based on four broad categories of behavior (Lewis, 2002). Observers look for examples related to focal questions in each of the following categories:

1. Academic learning: How do students draw on course material in their discussion? Where do they get stuck or confused?
2. Motivation and engagement: Do particular students disengage from the group or task? What can I tell about student motivation based on tone of voice, persistence, and comments?
3. Social behavior: In what ways do students challenge and support one another throughout the task? In what ways do they work constructively toward the task goal? What do they do that impedes working toward the task goal? Do students assume roles in their group such as leader, note taker, or time keeper?
4. Student attitudes toward learning: Do students maintain interest in the activity throughout the period? What positive or negative comments do they make about the task?

These four categories of behavior encompass a broad range and satisfy my goal of casting a wide net. An advantage of this four-category framework is that it reduces the cognitive load on observers, which makes note-taking more manageable. Instead of trying to record everything students do and say, observers can focus on certain types of behavior.

Second, to look more carefully at students' interactions, I use a checklist of behaviors that typify successful and unsuccessful group learning. For example, in effective groups, participants ask and answer questions, use evidence to support ideas, and ask for and give examples. In unproductive groups, members tend to interrupt one another, criticize others, change the subject often, make frequent irrelevant comments, and make unsupported claims. In the class observation, observers can use the checklist to note the frequency of each type of productive and counterproductive behavior.

I now have two viable observation protocols: One focuses broadly on student learning, motivation, attitudes, and social behavior, and the other focuses on specific behaviors that support or impede group learning. Fortunately, I can use both. Four colleagues volunteered to serve as observers, so two will use the four-category protocol, and two will use the group behavior checklist protocol.

Whom to Observe

Each of my 4 colleagues will observe a group of 16 to 20 students for the entire class period, which is about half the class. Observing a representative sample of students is good practice. However, in our classes we have samples of convenience—our own students. Many variables could potentially influence student performance such as ability, interest, background knowledge of the topic, major, gender, year in school, and so on. If I plan to observe a sample of students in the class, I may want to arrange groups to meet the needs of the study. For example, if I think it is important to do so, I'll try to balance gender representation, student ability, or other factors of importance. In an exploratory study, though, I prefer for students to work in their regular groups.

Orient the Observers

Because the observers are vital to the success of the study, I prepare explicit instructions and guidelines for their roles. This is especially important when they haven't participated in planning the study. The information includes a synopsis of the study, its purpose, and what I hope to learn from it; a copy of the protocol observers will use with instructions about how to record information; and ground rules for observing (e.g., don't interact with students, refrain from answering questions, don't interrupt the groups to ask for clarification, allow the instructor to introduce observers and describe their role to the class).

If possible, I meet with observers prior to the class observation to review the study, walk through the protocol, discuss the ground rules, and answer questions about how to carry out the observation.

Prepare Students for the Observation

I prefer to explain the study to students and obtain informed consent prior to the scheduled observation of a class period. This allows time for students to ask questions and consider whether to grant informed consent. On the day of the observation, I remind students about the purpose of the study, reiterate confidentiality and anonymity concerns, and introduce the observers and describe their role in the class.

I try to normalize the event by emphasizing that the class is no different from other class days except that observers will watch several groups, and the students do not need to do anything special or out of the ordinary. I also emphasize that in addition to the specific purpose of the study, my goal as an instructor is to use information from classroom research to try to improve my teaching and better support their learning.

I am sometimes asked whether the presence of observers influences students' thinking and behavior. The answer, of course, is yes. The important concern is whether observer presence matters and if it changes student behavior significantly. Students may be more sensitive to outside observers in certain circumstances, such as when they might be asked to disclose personal information or discuss controversial topics. But in many classrooms, observers are likely to have a minimal effect on students. A number of strategies can help reduce the possibility of bias. One strategy is for observers to note instances where they suspect that students are acting differently because of their presence, and then discuss it with other observers and decide on the extent of bias. A second strategy is to survey students after the class and ask them about their reactions to having observers in the class. A third, preventive, strategy is to desensitize students to observer presence by asking colleagues to attend the class several times prior to the study observation. Students tend to acclimate quickly to the presence of observers.

Carry Out the Observation

Being an observer is like sitting in a fast-paced lecture. It can be difficult to keep up and record a faithful representation of the events. At the end of an observation, I try to sit down for 5 to 10 minutes to review my notes and fill in the gaps before I forget the details.

Observation should entail pure description separate from inferences about the meaning of the observation. As a classroom teacher, it's hard for me not to interpret as I observe. I do this automatically in class. I listen to a student's question and immediately make assumptions about the student's point of view and how he or she developed it. Part of this impulse comes from hearing the same questions over many years of teaching. I may have a ready-made explanation or theory to account for students' comments. As an observer, I may not be able to suppress the impulse to interpret the behavior I observe, but being aware that I am doing so can help me differentiate between what I observe and what I think it means. As an observer, my job is to describe what students do and say. Later, when the observers discuss their observations, I have a chance to express my interpretations and explain the behavior I observed.

Expect Surprises

Not everything that happens in a class period will fit the protocol. Some interesting and important things happen unexpectedly. I was an observer for a classroom study in which students worked in groups. I observed one group and sat among the six group members for the entire class period. Ten minutes into the class, the group members were completely disengaged from the assigned task and involved in side conversations, homework for other classes, and the like. The group never worked on the task at all. At the end of the class period, each group reported on their work. In my group, a student volunteered to give the summary report after four or five other groups had given their reports. He simply reiterated what students before him had said. The students in this group not only failed to work on the task but also learned nothing and then presented a summary that made it seem like they had diligently done their work. The instructor was completely unaware of the situation, and this observation led to radical revisions in the organization and facilitation of group tasks in the class.

Organize and Analyze Results

In this exploratory study, I collect two sources of observational data about student learning and behavior: one based on the checklist, and the other based on open-ended written observations. The checklist data indicate the frequency of various student behaviors and depict how students interacted in their groups during the class period. The second source of information is detailed notes by two observers about students' learning, motivation and engagement, social behavior, and attitudes toward the experience. In addition to observational data, I can use students' written summaries (individual and group) as evidence of what they learned during the group tasks.

A first step in data analysis is to meet with all the observers to discuss their observations and interpretations of student learning and behavior. Typically, discussion of an exploratory study is wide-ranging. Observers highlight important themes and patterns, point out unique or unexpected findings, and may discuss the behavior of individual students in detail.

Following the discussion with observers, I summarize the checklists and notes. I also assess students' written summaries.

Based on the data, I can compare my model of productive discussions with how students actually interacted with one another. In doing this I simply look for patterns: What are the most frequent types of productive and counterproductive behaviors? Do some groups look more effective or ineffective than others based on their level of productive and counterproductive behavior? Are certain types of behavior especially salient in terms of either facilitating or impeding discussion? Did groups that interacted productively learn more (reflected in the written summaries) than groups that were more unproductive?

In an exploratory study, I am not trying to confirm a specific hypothesis. Instead, I want to use the data to provide detailed descriptions of what group learning looked like in the class. The results are a combination of information that is quantitative (e.g., the number of times students interact in particular ways) and qualitative (e.g., predominant themes and patterns and examples that illustrate specific types of behavior).

The observational study provides a rich, detailed picture of how students interact in a group learning situation, which is a source of new ideas about the factors that support and impede group learning. With greater insight into group learning processes, I am in a better position to propose strategies to support effective group learning.

The 18-minute film Can You Lift 100KG? *(Lewis, 2000) depicts fifth-grade Japanese elementary teachers planning, teaching, observing, and analyzing a class lesson on the science of levers.*

The observation study serves as an essential precursor to implementing and studying the effectiveness of teaching practices for group learning.

When to Choose Classroom Observation

A major aim of SoTL is to explain how and why students learn or don't learn what we teach them. Classroom observation is essential if the goal is to focus on learning processes and not solely on the products of learning. Observation works best when students externalize their thinking through discussion, writing, drawing, thinking aloud, and the like. By observing students as they engage in a learning task, we can identify their paths to solving a problem or formulating an idea, how they use background knowledge, interpret new information, make decisions, where and how they have difficulty, and so forth.

Observation can also play a key role in understanding interactions between teaching and learning. Traditional classroom observations focus almost exclusively on the instructor. In SoTL, we want to understand how teaching affects learning, in terms of not only what students learn but also how teaching facilitates and supports learning.

I believe that using classroom observation as a method of inquiry can have an important side effect. The practice of observing in the classroom promotes cognitive empathy, the capacity to see the subject matter from students' perspectives. As experts, we may have difficulty remembering what it's like not to know our subject matter. We know the subject so well it may not occur to us that novices don't know the subject at all and may struggle to understand it. These *expert blind spots*, as they are called, prevent us from understanding what it's like to grapple with the subject matter. Teachers report that the experience of observing attunes them to how students think about concepts and skills (Cerbin, 2011).

The time needed to carry out extensive observations is a limitation of observation as a method of inquiry. For that reason, observation may be most useful for pilot studies to gain insight into the variables we want to study and in specific contexts such as single-class lessons that involve brief teaching and learning episodes.

Observing brings us closer to the contexts and processes at play as students learn. We can watch as students learn on their own or with others and how they respond to instruction. Understanding how teaching and learning work is an important foundation for subsequent SoTL experiences to identify ways to advance teaching and learning, and observation is a bridge that can connect our curiosity, hunches, and suspicions about student performance to the actual processes involved in learning.

References

Cerbin, B. (2011). *Lesson study: Using classroom inquiry to improve teaching and learning in higher education*. Sterling, VA: Stylus.

Cerbin, B. (2013). Emphasizing learning in the scholarship of teaching and learning, *International Journal for the Scholarship of Teaching and Learning, 7*(1), Article 5. doi:10.20429/ijsotl.2013.070105

Lewis, C. (Producer). (2000). *Can you lift 100kg? [video]*. Retrieved from http://www.lessonresearch.net/canyoulift1.html

Lewis, C. (2002). Lesson study: A handbook of teacher-led instructional improvement. Philadelphia, PA: Research for Better Schools.

Nuthall, G. (2007). *The hidden lives of learners.* Wellington, New Zealand: NZCER Press.

Perkins, D. (2007). Theories of difficulty. In N. Entwistle & P. Tomlinson (Eds.), Student learning and university teaching (pp. 31–48). Leicester, England: British Psychological Society.

CONDUCTING INTERVIEWS

Capturing What Is Unobserved

Janice Miller-Young

In order to understand other persons' constructions of reality, we would do well to ask them . . . and to ask them in such a way that they can tell us in their terms (rather than those imposed rigidly and a priori by ourselves) and in a depth which addresses the rich context that is the substance of their meanings. (Jones, 1985, p. 46)

An interview is an opportunity for the scholarship of teaching and learning (SoTL) researchers to focus on understanding their students better and what they are experiencing in their learning. However, getting good data from interviewing requires asking good questions, and asking good questions takes practice. As an engineer, when I first engaged in SoTL, I was skeptical about interviews. I feared my inexperience with qualitative research could introduce bias, that I might unknowingly ask leading questions in an interview, and that I would just generally influence the data in ways I was not comfortable with or might not even be aware of. I've since used and participated in interviews and realized that an interview is not only an adaptable, flexible data collection tool but also a systematic activity that can be learned through practice, reflection, and feedback. So in this chapter I discuss not only important considerations for conducting SoTL research interviews but also strategies for learning how to do them well, which are just as important.

Benefits of SoTL Interviews

Interviews can be used to gain rich insights into students' knowledge, experiences, perceptions, and feelings. Incorporating interviews into a SoTL study can be a positive experience for the instructor and students. Interviewing students gives instructors an opportunity to listen and learn from students, and it gives students an opportunity to reflect on their learning, voice their perspectives on teaching and learning, and offer suggestions for improvement to a course or program. A good interview also allows unexpected information to emerge and be explored, a key benefit of qualitative methods.

Often when I work with instructors who are designing a SoTL study, I recommend including interviews in the study design, especially if they are intending to collect quantitative data using an instrument that has not been validated, such as a self-created rubric or survey. Adding interviews, which is using mixed methods, is one way strengthen such a study's findings. Sometimes instructors are quite convinced they will see significant differences in a quantitative measure such as test scores or survey responses as a result of some change to their teaching. I encourage them to ask themselves, What if I don't see a significant difference? Or any difference? What could be some possible reasons for that? and What if I do see a difference? What would I want to know more about in terms of explaining why there is difference? Then I suggest that an interview could help them explore those reasons.

Of course it's not as simple as just adding an interview to an otherwise existing research design. Like all research, data-gathering strategies in interviews must align with the goals of the study. Whether we are interested in the cognitive or affective domain of students' learning, a good interview protocol will include questions that elicit more than simply students' self-reported perceptions of their learning or their perceptions of which course activities most influenced their learning.

Students' knowledge can be classified as semantic (knowing facts, meanings, concepts), procedural (knowing how to do something), integrative (being able to connect and synthesize multiple knowledge models), or metacognitive (being able to think about and control one's cognitive and learning processes). Whichever aspect is of interest, it is important to develop interview questions that require students to demonstrate that kind of knowledge. Questions should generate responses that can be critically analyzed for their level of understanding or application of concepts or that illuminate their thinking process. Questions about how students do something, and which refer to concrete events or ideas, can be useful, such as, Can you tell me how . . . ? Can you walk me through the process you used to . . . ? or How would you respond to the view that . . . ? At the same time, interview responses may be filtered by students' expectations of what they think we want to hear and are representative of their thinking at only one point in time. Thus, it is best to triangulate interview results about student knowledge with other sources of data. Many possible data sources are available to us as SoTL researchers. Course artifacts such as discussion board postings, assignments, and exam questions are just a few. For example, in a SoTL study with my engineering class on how students visualized two-dimensional drawings of three-dimensional structures, I discovered some themes about what students were struggling with through interviews. I analyzed their submitted course work and found evidence of the same struggles in some of their written problem-solving approaches as well, strengthening my conviction that the interview results were representative of what students struggled with in the course (Miller-Young, 2013).

Interviews allow us to capture data that cannot be observed, and thus they are particularly good for exploring the affective domain of student learning, such as their attitudes, beliefs, and motivations about the course content, teaching strategies used, their discipline, or learning in general. One might also ask about factors that may influence students' learning, such as values, social pressures, stereotypes, or anxiety. If one of these aspects is what we want to know about, we may decide that interviewing will be the primary mode of data collection. Open-ended prompts and questions that yield descriptive stories about students' experiences, opinions, and feelings work well, for example, "Tell me about a time when . . . . Can you give me an example of . . . ? Tell me more about that . . . . What was it like for you when . . . ?" (Merriam, 2009, p. 99). Questions like these also convey to interviewees that the interviewer is genuinely interested in their thoughts and experiences, thus building rapport and eliciting richer responses.

Preparing and Practicing Interview Questions

Most SoTL studies benefit from semistructured interviews (Webb, 2015) in which a list of questions is prepared in advance to ensure the interview is focused enough to answer the research question. The interviewer also has the flexibility to respond to new ideas or issues as they arise, through probing and follow-up questions or even exploring unanticipated ideas through new questions.

In developing a list of questions or issues to be explored, I like to start with several specific questions I make sure I ask everyone and that are strongly aligned with the research question (see chapter 6). Perspectives based on my own experience, other studies, and theories help frame these questions. I might also prepare some open-ended questions with probes. Generally it's good to start with relatively neutral and descriptive questions at the beginning, such as, Tell me about your experience learning to work in teams, which invite the interviewee to start to describe the topic of interest, make the interviewee comfortable, and establish a rapport. The questions can then

A study by Cooper, Ashley, and Brownell (2016) nicely illustrated a semi-structured interview process. This study investigated the influence of a summer bridge program to help students make the transition from high school to introductory biology in college. The authors described how pilot exploratory interviews unexpectedly found that students who participated in a summer bridge program had sophisticated views of active learning, which they then wanted to explore further. Thirty-four semistructured interviews were conducted with Bridge students as well as students who were eligible for but did not participate in the program. Interviews were conducted while they were taking the college course and were the only source of data. The article included exemplar quotes to illustrate the common themes that emerged; some of the interview excerpts also included interviewer questions and illustrated how open-ended, follow-up questions can help get richer or clarifying information from interviewees. The study concluded that the bridge program positively affected student attitudes and self-reported behaviors related to active learning compared to those of similar students who did not participate.

become more focused such as, What factors do you see as causing conflict on your team? Thinking about what not to ask is also useful. For example, Why? questions are less effective because they tend to lead to speculation or make people defensive. It is easy to imagine that asking someone, Why did you try to solve the problem that way? might make him or her feel awkward or defensive. Asking multiple questions at the same time, leading questions, and questions that can be answered by yes or no should also be avoided. Further guidance on the technical details of interview structure and types of questions is available elsewhere; see, for example, Bishop-Clark and Dietz-Uhler (2012) and Merriam (2009).

After drafting the guiding questions, I next practice the interview. This process is critical and can be a learning experience in itself for novice and experienced interviewers. I first review the questions by posing them to myself. Are there any that would make me feel uncomfortable to answer? Are there any that are too detailed, too leading, or can be answered by yes or no? I'll also pilot test the interview with a student, checking to see if it's clear to the interviewee what is being asked. Does the student's body language seem to indicate that my questioning makes him or her feel valued rather than interrogated? I use my list as a guide but I also go with the flow, changing the wording and order of questions to fit the conversation. I may even conduct more than one pilot interview, each time reflecting on the extent of sponta-neous, rich, specific, and relevant answers they elicit from the interviewees; the degree to which the questions are shorter than the students' answers; which questions seem to elicit interesting or unexpected responses; and the degree to which the students' responses are clear (Kvale, 1996). In fact, I'll continue to reflect on these indicators of interview quality throughout the entire study, recursively refining my questions during and after each inter-view. For novice interviewers, a community of practice is also a useful way to develop, practice, and reflect on an interview protocol, adding the benefit of multiple perspectives on the process and the opportunity to be interviewee as well (Miller-Young & Boman, 2017). Being interviewed, whether by an experienced or novice interviewer, can be a valuable way to learn how the interviewer's behavior can influence the thoughts and emotions of the inter-viewee (Hsiung, 2008). As a more confident interviewer who is genuinely interested in participants' perspectives, I now look forward to listening and responding to an interview as it unfolds, probing for more detail or clarifica-tion and being surprised by new and unexpected ideas that may emerge.

Conducting the Interviews

In addition to planning and practicing the questions, a number of other important and interrelated aspects about conducting SoTL interviews should be considered. How many students will be interviewed? How often and when? Who will conduct the interviews? As a researcher, I keep the question and philosophical approach in mind in making such decisions, but as a teacher I also consider my relationship with my students and how to maintain it or even strengthen it through a well-executed study.

How Many Students Will Be Interviewed?

This depends on the interest in breadth versus depth. To understand the vari-ety of experiences of students in a large class, 20 to 50 interviews using a pur-poseful sample makes sense. For in-depth case studies, interviewing a single student may be appropriate. For small classes in which the researcher has a good relationship with students who feel strongly about contributing, all of them might be interviewed. Usually, I plan to interview as many of the stu-dents who volunteer as possible, making it clear in advance that interviews will continue until saturation is reached (no new information is emerging from the interviews), so that some students aren't left wondering why they didn't have the opportunity to participate. One of my experienced colleagues says she always knows when she's finished interviewing because she starts to get bored.

Corbett (2015) illustrated how interviewing can be an effective tech-nique when conducting intensive case studies of just a few individuals. The author described how he observed the connections between a learning disabled (LD) student and a course-based peer tutor in a first-year composi-tion course. The author was not the instructor for the course, but recruited for and coordinated the peer tutoring program, and thus was able to do classroom observations followed by in-depth interviews. With thoughtful and rich narrative, the author described not only the compelling stories of the student's and peer tutor's struggles with their LDs, which were revealed during the interviews, but also the many times he was surprised by what he heard. The appreciative tone and rapport he developed through his inter-views was evidenced by the fact that when he indicated to the student inter-viewee that the interview was complete, the student continued to offer his reflections, emphasizing what he thought were the most difficult struggles he had experienced. The author concluded his study with a deeper appre-ciation of "what it means to struggle, to persevere, and to make the most of what 'others' of all backgrounds and abilities have to offer" (p. 471). He also described the ethical dilemmas he struggled with throughout the research process, being particularly worried about the potential to objec-tify or victimize the LD student. It is interesting to note that when he asked the student to review the manuscript before submitting it, the stu-dent responded with enthusiasm about how touched he was to have such a detailed description of his experiences be respectfully shared with others and how he felt honored to have been part of the research.

How Often and When?

Often SoTL researchers wait until the end of a course so they can conduct the interviews themselves, but there are considerations other than simply convenience. If the impact of a particular teaching strategy is of interest, interviewing students as soon as possible after the learning experience or later to assess learning or change over the long term will be useful. If in-depth, narrative accounts or changes over time are of interest, multiple interviews might be appropriate. For studies in which themes are allowed to emerge from the data, it is good practice to check one's interpretations of initial interview responses with a follow-up interview, building trustworthiness into the study while also maintaining the trust of students. In reality, sometimes constraints such as resources, scheduling, and sheer numbers of participants dictate how often and when interviews will take place, and we must make the best of it and acknowledge the limitations.

Who Conducts the Interviews?

SoTL researchers often conduct interviews themselves, as their deep familiarity with the research question and context allows them to probe and respond to unanticipated information effectively. It can also be a way to show students that we care and want to learn from them. Other considerations include the sensitivity of the topic and whether students might be more forthcoming if their identity was not attached to their comments, at least for the instructor. Deciding whether the instructor or someone at arm's length from the interviewees would be a more appropriate interviewer is a judgement call that will likely be influenced by the instructor's disciplinary training and worldview. Training student research assistants to be interviewers can resolve these tensions. Senior students who have taken the course or similar courses are well positioned to be interviewers; however, they still require from the instructor a significant investment of time for training, particularly for less structured interviews. Thus, for a small number of interviews and for instructors who want to take a very exploratory approach, conducting interviews themselves often makes sense. When a large number of interviews will be conducted, it is worth the time to hire and train an interviewer. Good training requires creating opportunities for trainees to practice, conducting the first few interviews with them, gradually giving them more agency during interviews, and monitoring and analyzing the interview process together as the study progresses. Although time intensive, it is a valuable process.

Closing Thoughts

Interviewing is a valuable way to understand students' experiences and perspectives, and it can be used in SoTL studies with a wide range of questions and research approaches. Practicing and gathering data through interviews is a time-intensive and sometimes ethically challenging process; however, it allows us to see what is otherwise unobservable, and the richness of data that interviews can generate is more than worth the effort. This richness helps to not only advance our collective understanding of teaching and learning but also share compelling stories that challenge our assumptions about the realities and experiences of our students. Beyond these benefits, an interviewer who is flexible and responsive to unexpected information elicited from students effectively allows students to move from being passive research participants to active contributors in the research process. It is one important way to give students agency and voice in what is attended to in researching and also in practicing teaching in higher education.

References

Bishop-Clark, C., & Dietz-Uhler, B. (2012). *Engaging in the scholarship of teaching and learning: A guide to the process, and how to develop a project from start to finish.* Sterling, VA: Stylus.

Cooper, K. M., Ashley, M., & Brownell, S. E. (2016). A bridge to active learning: A summer bridge program helps students maximize their active-learning experiences and the active-learning experiences of others. *CBE–Life Sciences Education, 16*(1), Article 17.

Corbett, S. J. (2015). Learning disability and response-ability reciprocal caring in developmental peer response writing groups and beyond. *Pedagogy, 15,* 459–475.

Hsiung, P. C. (2008). Teaching reflexivity in qualitative interviewing. *Teaching Sociology, 36,* 211–226.

Jones, S. (1985). Depth interviewing. In R. Walker (Ed.), *Applied qualitative research* (pp. 45–55). Aldershot, Hampshire, England: Gower.

Kvale, S. (1996). *InterViews: An introduction to qualitative research interviewing.* Thousand Oaks, CA: Sage.

Merriam, S. B. (2009). *Qualitative research: A guide to design and implementation.* San Francisco, CA: Jossey-Bass.

Miller-Young, J. (2013). Calculations and expectations: How engineering students describe three-dimensional forces. *Canadian Journal for the Scholarship of Teaching and Learning, 4*(1). Retrieved from http://dx.doi.org/10.5206/cjsotl-rca-cea.2013.1.4

Miller-Young, J. & Boman, J. (Eds.). (2017). *Using the decoding the disciplines framework for learning across disciplines.* San Francisco, CA: Jossey-Bass.

Webb, A. (2015). Research interviews in the scholarship of teaching and learning. *Transformative Dialogues, 8*(1). Retrieved from http://www.kpu.ca/sites/default/files/Transformative%20Dialogues/TD.8.1.9_Webb_Research_Interviews.pdf

II

CLOSE READING

Paying Attention to Student Artifacts

Karen Manarin

I still remember the moment I realized I could use my disciplinary skills as an English scholar and teacher to do the scholarship of teaching and learning (SoTL). It was a huge relief because it meant I didn't have to give up my underlying belief that language shapes rather than merely records experience; I didn't have to rely on quantitative measures to adequately represent the vagaries of student learning. I could do close readings of student work.

But what is close reading exactly? Some people assume it just means talking about the details of a text, but it's more than that. Close reading involves paying attention to what was said and how it was said to increase our understanding about something. Sometimes people complain that close reading involves reading too much into the text, that is, making it mean whatever we want. Trying to avoid this situation, literary theorist Scholes (2002) emphasized the need for distance in close reading:

> [read] as if the words belonged to a person at some distance from ourselves in thought or feeling. Perhaps they must be seen as the words of someone else before they can be seen as words at all—or, more particularly, as words that need to be read with close attention. (p. 166)

Doing a close reading means being willing to consider multiple interpretations of text, even those that don't seem immediately obvious to us because of our assumptions. Bass and Linkon (2008) discuss close reading in terms of inquiry, a framework that may be more familiar to SoTL practitioners:

Close reading integrates four elements: inquiry, texts, theory, and argument. Literary analysis begins with inquiry, often based on an observation. What does this pattern mean? What might we gain by reading this text through this lens? How do the multiple layers of meaning within a text contradict and vex it in culturally meaningful ways? How does one text influence another? Projects end with argument, the detailed explication of a reading that theorizes about the text and extends and refines theory based on that reading. Literary arguments gain validity when they are grounded in careful attention to texts and engaged with theory. The phrase "close reading" may seem to imply primary emphasis on the text itself, but the examination of text occurs within and gains significance only when it is embedded in inquiry, engages with theory and generates an argument that is useful to other readers. (p. 247)

I think the last part is the hardest. The argument, typically about what a particular passage of text means or why it was written in a specific way, has to be useful to other readers. Poor close reading focuses so exclusively on the details of the particular text that no one else cares about the interpretation. A good close reading of a particular text provides a reason someone else should care about the interpretation; the interpretation contributes to readers' understanding of something beyond that passage by providing insight that could be useful in other texts and contexts.

As a literary scholar, I read literature closely. I identify patterns and variation from patterns, I consider the author's historical and cultural context, and I select details to support an informed interpretation of a particular text. My analysis of text is like a case study that if done well suggests something about other texts or contexts. For example, my close reading of an eighteenth-century poem may reveal something about how the author wrote other poems or perhaps about how people in that time period responded to an issue or idea.

As a SoTL scholar, I read all sorts of student assignments closely, their essays, journals, in-class writings, exams that aren't multiple choice, even assignments with visual components like research posters (Manarin, 2016). Indeed, given what we know about semiotics (the exploration of how meaning is constructed and communicated through signs), it's possible to read drawings, photographs, performances, sculpture, web design, music, interior design, and more, depending on context (Chandler, 1994).

My focus is really on the written texts or artifacts students produce. When I am doing a close reading of student work, I identify patterns and variation from patterns, I consider my institutional context, and I select details to support an informed interpretation about student learning. I hope my interpretation about student learning will be useful to other people in other

Wineburg (2001) explored the cognitive framework involved in learning to think like a historian. This collection included several essays demonstrating close reading of student artifacts. He evaluated pictures drawn by schoolchildren, responses to historical documents by high school students, and interviews with working historians as he argued for the importance of recognizing the past as alien to ourselves.

contexts and classes, even though I know it cannot be generalized to all students. That limitation, however, is not something specific to close reading. After all, as Grauerholz and Main (2013) noted when talking about fallacies of SoTL, teaching involves "social acts informed by cultural traditions that become most meaningful when described in terms of specific histories and larger social contexts" (p. 158).

Sometimes SoTL practitioners talk about needing evidence of student learning. I think of this evidence in terms of artifacts students create. I like the idea of artifacts because it points to several important assumptions. Whatever a student writes or draws or performs (for the rest of this chapter I focus on writing) is shaped by a series of choices the student made. Some of these choices are individual, some are shaped by context and genre. For example, a student who writes a research paper is working within a framework set by the instructor's expectations for that particular assignment. For instance, I expect a research paper to be documented in a particular way, be a specific length, and contain a certain number of sources; it might even have been written on a topic from an approved list. Within that framework, however, the student makes choices about what to include and exclude. Some of those choices are shaped by what the student thinks the instructor might want, and some are shaped by the student's experience, so it's possible to see traces of all sorts of things in the artifact. But the artifact is not an unmediated representation of the writer's reality, nor does it represent the writer forever. It's a set of choices that occurs in a particular time and context; in another context or at another time, the choices would probably be different. And my context matters too: A different reader may very well notice other elements or reach different conclusions. However, this doesn't mean the reading is invalid, it means the reading process is complex.

Literary theorist Rosenblatt (1978/1994) talked about reading as a transaction among writer, text, and reader. The reader constructs meaning of the text rather than finding the meaning hidden in the text. To be meaningful, then, the artifact requires someone to interpret, to read closely. I would argue this reading should be more nuanced than a basic content analysis. How something is written is important. Writers emphasize some details, but they leave out others. They use different rhetorical strategies. They make assumptions about their readers. Close reading requires us to consider the relationship among writer, text, and reader. Iser (1978) argued that a writer imagines an implied reader, anticipating and trying to provoke particular responses. A real reader experiences the tension between his or her experiences and the text's expectations. Close reading involves exploring these areas of tension to create meaning. For example, the

Chick, Hassel, and Haynie (2009) described a lesson study about Theodore Roethke's poem "My Papa's Waltz." They collected initial responses before using an annotation exercise with transparencies in class to explore the poem. Students were then asked to write another response. They provided close readings of all three types of artifacts, valuing the complexity of the students' responses.

male student who writes about feminism, saying, "If I wanted to hear someone bitch, I would listen to my mother more" wants his female instructor (probably the same age as his mother) to know he is resistant to the ideas. He is challenging her. But what if the same statement was written for a male instructor? If the text is addressed to a woman (particularly the woman who assigned the reading), he wants to provoke, but if addressed to a man, he wants perhaps to provoke, perhaps to bond with his reader over the shrewishness of women. Would the same statement even be written for a male instructor? What if the writer is a woman? Does that change the dynamic? How? Asking these sorts of questions about an artifact can provide glimpses of student thinking.

Doing a close reading of student artifacts for a SoTL project is different from marking assignments in the context of the class. When I'm marking students' work, I am evaluating the particular artifact on multiple measures against a set of outcomes. When I'm doing a close reading, I'm not usually evaluating anything; I'm just looking for patterns in a response or set of responses. I usually begin by looking at a content area (what was said or demonstrated in the artifact), and then I move to how it was said or demonstrated. Sometimes I look at what wasn't said because paying attention to the silences can be important (Jackson & Mazzei, 2012). Often I read something in multiple ways, "with" and "against" the grain (Bartholomae & Petrosky, 1999, p. 11). Reading with the grain means reading as the writer hoped the reader would, trying to understand what the writer wanted the reader to see in his or her own terms. Reading against the grain, in contrast, is a type of resistance reading, considering the unexamined assumptions, contradictions, or silences of an artifact.

Salvatori and Donahue (2004) provided close readings of students engaged with difficult texts and promoted the idea of a difficulty paper in which students explore what they find difficult about a particular text. Students described how they attempted to solve the difficulty and reflected on what they have learned. Each chapter was built on close readings of these difficulty papers.

Artifacts then can be oblique measures of student learning, but examining artifacts involves interpretation. In SoTL this interpretation is then communicated to others who also have to interpret and decide whether the interpretation is meaningful. My interpretation is acceptable, not necessarily if other people agree with me (although that is always nice) but if they take me seriously enough to consider it (Fish, 1980). I need to explain my assumptions and context and provide enough detail in my close reading so that readers of my work can decide whether my interpretations are meaningful in their contexts. Also, I cannot rely exclusively on paraphrase and summary; I need specific quotations immediately followed by analysis.

This is probably why I find it difficult when writing for a SoTL journal to separate the findings from the discussion, sections commonly found in many social science articles. That organizational pattern doesn't lend itself well to close reading because there is too much of a gap between the specific quotations from the artifacts and my interpretation of what those quotations mean. The quotations from student work are treated like raw data that can be objectively discussed later, an epistemological assumption that runs through a number of social science approaches. For example, Merriam and Tisdell (2016) talk about "mining data from documents and artifacts" (p. 162), as if meaning is just sitting there waiting to be unearthed, but close reading constructs meaning. I find it much easier to combine findings and the discussion, an organizational pattern that allows me to show and tell my reader my interpretations of the learning glimpsed through student artifacts. I want to give my reader the chance to see what I saw, but I also want to explain the inferences I drew from those specific words presented in that specific way. When I am doing a close reading of student work, the analysis starts when I first read the work, and it doesn't end until my text has been written and rewritten through however many drafts. I cannot just write the results of the study. The act of writing shapes those results, as my choices in writing an article come to together to form an artifact that has to be interpreted by my reader.

An example might help explain what close reading is and isn't. A few years ago, my colleagues and I were examining how students read in four different first-year general education courses (Manarin, Carey, Rathburn, and Ryland, 2015). Students in each course wrote reading responses, which we gathered and measured against a set of hybridized rubrics based on the Valid Assessment of Learning in Undergraduate Education (VALUE) rubrics (Association of American Colleges & Universities, 2009). We were making complex qualitative judgments about whether the reading responses, our artifacts, showed traces of student learning in terms of categories like comprehension and analysis. We were reading the work carefully, but I wouldn't describe it as close reading because we were primarily interested in whether the student work demonstrated particular markers as articulated on our rubrics. Certainly when we were describing our results, we would pick a representative quotation and explain why we put it in one category or another by pointing out particular details, but the categories were largely a priori. It was a deductive approach.

When we started to work with our hybridized rubric for critical reading for social engagement, however, we found that most of the student work wasn't described by our rubric. It wasn't just that the students were failing to achieve the descriptors for civic engagement, they seemed to be doing something different. So we went back to the reading responses to try to describe what we saw. It was an inductive process. At first glance (and second and third) we saw an overwhelming variety of responses because the content areas were so diverse, everything from scientific literacy through composition. Students were writing in response to readings about climate change, genocide, the democratic process, feminism, AIDS, and so on. Simply doing a content analysis according to generic or basic qualitative methodology, where we would code and recode, collapsing categories into larger themes (Merriam & Tisdell, 2016), wasn't going to get us very far. It could tell us what the topics were, but we already knew that. After all, we had assigned the readings in the first place. So we went back to the reading responses and started to read, looking not for content but for what the writers seemed to be doing when they wrote about content: Did they read the assigned text (as far as we could tell from details provided)? Did they identify a specific issue discussed in the assigned text? How did they do that? Did they link it to other issues or other texts? If they didn't identify an issue, what did they do instead? How did the particular context of the class, and the students' expectations, shape the response (as far as we could tell)? Did they express emotion? What emotion? How did we know? What was the tone of the reading response? How did the students position their readers in the text; for example, did they want to provoke or did they assume agreement? Did the students generalize when talking about the reading? What did that look like? What details from the reading did they think were important enough to include? What details did they leave out? Could we tell why? Were there patterns among students' or in one student's responses over time? Because we were interested here in critical reading for social engagement, how, if at all, did they position themselves in the world? Did they assume some agency, or did they describe themselves as helpless in the face of larger social forces? Each of these questions required us to read closely, to pay attention not just to what was said (or not said) but also to how it was said.

Close reading requires rereading the artifacts multiple times, sometimes with the grain, sometimes against the grain. It also requires making a lot of notes or annotations. For the critical reading project, we read through the responses, noting more questions than answers. We read again trying to decide what details we, or our peers, would find convincing in answering any of these questions. We read again, dwelling on those responses where students seemed to include a lot of details or express emotion. We highlighted, underlined, used colored sticky notes, wrote in margins, wrote in journals, drew patterns, and eventually wound up with what we called a *taxonomy of absence*, a flow chart that seemed to describe the ways our students weren't doing what we expected them to do. We then went back to the artifacts, looking to see if we had described most of them, examining the outliers again.

For this project, we didn't use a qualitative software tool like NVivo (www.qsrinternational.com/nvivo/nvivo-products), but I think it's possible to do a close reading using that sort of tool. Sometimes people assume these tools do the analysis, but they are really just a way of organizing data. People still have to read and interpret. I think success using something like NVivo for close reading would depend on two main factors: coding beyond content and paying attention to context. Someone would still have to read through the artifacts multiple times, coding for particular ways the material was written. They would also want to always check for the context around any quotations pulled; after all, it's much easier to recognize how a particular quotation fits into an artifact when glancing at the whole page. NVivo is the electronic equivalent of colored markers and sticky notes, but it is important to remember that it can't take the place of our brains.

When writing our argument, we had to provide enough details for our readers to understand and judge our interpretation so they, too, could read with and against the grain. For the decision points, we provided quotations from the student artifacts followed by analysis; we wanted to persuade our readers about our interpretation. We also suggested alternative interpretations and admitted ignorance. We don't know for sure why our students wrote the way they did, and we don't know what or if they learned. All we have are our interpretations, supported by nuanced, careful, and repeated reading of artifacts. These interpretations are based on our experience and our assumptions. The interpretations created through close reading are always contingent on the interpreter, but that doesn't mean that all interpretation, or all close reading, is equal. Close readings are meaningful when they contribute to our theory and practice, that is, when they help us see something we didn't see before. Close readings in SoTL need to be useful for people beyond the context of the class that generated the artifacts.

Close reading is a powerful method, but it requires comfort with constructivism, the idea that people construct knowledge of external reality through experience and reflection (Elliot, Fairweather, Olsen, & Pampaka, 2016). If someone really wants to objectively measure a change in behavior, close reading isn't the approach to take. Because SoTL is interdisciplinary, it's important to consider what elements a particular audience will find convincing. People of some disciplines will find close reading more persuasive than others, just as some will find statistically significant data more persuasive than others. When done well, close reading offers a way to examine the ambiguities of text, which, I suggest, makes it a wonderful method for exploring teaching and learning because learning is rarely unambiguous. Student-produced artifacts can provide glimpses of learning, but only if we slow down enough to look closely.

References

Association of American Colleges & Universities. (2009). *Assessing outcomes and improving achievement: Tips and tools for using rubrics*. Washington DC: Author.

Bartholomae, D., and Petrosky, A. (1999). *Ways of reading: An anthology for writers*. New York, NY: Bedford/St. Martin's.

Bass, R., & Linkon, S. L. (2008). On the evidence of theory: Close reading as a disciplinary model for writing about teaching and learning. *Arts and Humanities in Higher Education 7*, 245–261. doi:10.1177/1474022208094410

Chandler, D. (1994). *Semiotics for beginners*. Retrieved from http://visual-memory .co.uk/daniel/Documents/S4B/sem01.html

Chick, N., Hassel, H., & Haynie, A. (2009). Pressing an ear against the hive: Reading literature for complexity. *Pedagogy 9*, 399–422.

Elliot, M., Fairweather, I., Olsen, W., and Pampaka, M. (2016). *A dictionary of social science methods*. Oxford, England: Oxford University Press.

Fish, S. (1980). *Is there a text in this class: The authority of interpretative communities*. Cambridge, MA: Harvard University Press.

Grauerholz, L., & Main, E. (2013). Fallacies of SoTL: Rethinking how we conduct our research. In K. McKinney (Ed.), *The scholarship of teaching and learning in and across the disciplines* (pp. 152–168). Bloomington, IN: Indiana University Press.

Iser, W. (1978). *The act of reading: A theory of aesthetic response.* Baltimore, MD: Johns Hopkins University Press.

Jackson, A. Y., & Mazzei, L. A. (2012). *Thinking with theory in qualitative research: Viewing data across multiple perspectives.* New York, NY: Routledge.

Manarin, K. (2016). Interpreting undergraduate research posters in the literature classroom. *Teaching and Learning Inquiry, 4*(1). doi:10.20343/teachlearninqu .4.1.8

Manarin, K., Carey, M., Rathburn, M., & Ryland, G. (2015). *Critical reading for higher education: Academic goals and social engagement.* Bloomington, IN: Indiana University Press.

Merriam, S. B., & Tisdell, E. J. (2016). *Qualitative research: A guide to design and implementation.* San Francisco, CA: Wiley.

Rosenblatt, L. (1994). *The reader, the text, the poem: The transactional theory of the literary work.* Carbondale, IL: Southern Illinois University Press. (Original work published 1978).

Salvatori, M. R., & Donahue, P. (2004). *The elements (and pleasures) of difficulty.* New York, NY: Pearson.

Scholes, R. (2002). The transition to college reading. *Pedagogy, 2,* 165–172.

Wineburg, S. (2001). *Historical thinking and other unnatural acts.* Philadelphia, PA: Temple University Press.

STUDENT THINK-ALOUDS

Making Thinking and Learning Visible

Lendol Calder

What can think-alouds do for a scholarship of teaching and learning (SoTL) project? A lot perhaps, especially for those who can relate to the following anecdote.

> On a Sunday morning, my four-year-old daughter and I were in church. "Dear Lord," the minister began, with an upturned face and arms extended toward heaven. "Without you, we are but dust." She would have continued but at that moment my daughter looked up and in a bright, chirpy voice loud enough for everyone to hear asked, "Dad, what is butt dust?"

Butt dust—it is the axial problem of teaching and learning. I refer to the compound of misunderstandings, misreadings, misconceptions, rejections, persistent illusions, confusions, errors, terrors, half truths, and boo-boos that inevitably crop up when people are trying to make sense of new material. I suppose it won't do to call these things butt dust (it wouldn't be professional), but fortunately we can exhume an alternative term from an old medical dictionary that is equally descriptive: *brain lint*. Brain lint is a normal, natural, and necessary by-product of learning. The opposite of deep understanding, brain lint is maddeningly invisible to teachers, especially when we make the cognitive error of assuming, "I said it; that means they learned it." When student misunderstandings go unnoticed and uncorrected, brain lint accumulates in barren heaps and piles that yield a weedy harvest of learning failures.

I think we all know what I am talking about. A class flubs an assignment that was supposed to be easy. A prodigy in class discussions underperforms on her essays. Student researchers, warned repeatedly not to do so, continue to click on the first results returned by an Internet search query. Now and then, teachers see motes of brain lint floating in momentary sunbeams of enlightenment.

"How can I improve the grade on my essays?" a student asks. The question irks me.

"Did you read *any* of my comments?" I grump.

"Your comments don't make sense," he says, pulling a crumpled essay from his backpack. "Like, what does 'vagoo' mean? See—you wrote 'vagoo' here, here, and here."

"Vagoo?" I ask, tilting forward in my chair. Ah, it is undeniable. In the margin on every page I had scribbled *vague*. Beautiful, un-looked-for, dancing particles of brain lint!

Barzun (1945), that great teacher of teachers, observed that "the ideal aim of teaching is to have two minds share one thought" (p. 31). How depressing. If Barzun is correct, then call me an un-teacher, because what students think and what I think are, more often than not, miles apart. Steiner (2005), the fabled literary scholar, seconds Barzun and raises the bar. "The object of teaching," said Steiner, "is to build a community out of communication, a coherence of shared feelings, passions, refusals" (p. 26). Oh, that's not good. Because the refusals I see most often are students refusing to understand things I want them to learn. I think I am not alone in this. Eager to experience that community out of communication, what teacher in a moment of frustration hasn't wondered of students, *What* are they *thinking?!*

This is where think-alouds can help.

Think-aloud protocols are a research tool originally developed by cognitive psychologists to study a person's understanding of a concept, principle, or procedure. The basic idea behind a think-aloud is that if a subject can be trained to think out loud while completing a task, then the voiced introspections can be recorded, transcribed, and analyzed to determine what cognitive processes were in play. In disciplines as various as reading comprehension, mathematics, chemistry, and history, think-alouds have been used to identify what constitutes expert knowledge as compared to the thinking processes of nonexperts. For SoTL researchers, think-alouds can generate useful data for several kinds of questions.

Cognitive scientists use think-aloud protocol analyses to study human expertise, often comparing and contrasting how experts and novices solve complex problems (Wineburg, 1991). Calder (2006) demonstrated how think-alouds can be taken out of the laboratory and used in college classrooms to measure student learning over time.

For example, when observing a recurring bottleneck to learning, how does one identify the specific places where students get stuck? Or what about a teaching intervention or new course design: How effective for learning is the new approach, and what new moments of difficulty are created? A beautiful thing about think-alouds is how effective they are at uncovering and documenting what conventional assessment methods often miss—hidden levels of student insight and misunderstanding.

Cognitive psychologist Wineburg (1991) used think-aloud protocol analysis to compare how historians read historical texts with how high school students do the same. A classic example of an expert and novice research design for identifying what constitutes expertise in a domain of knowledge, Wineburg's think-aloud studies transformed the scholarship of teaching and learning in history.

The benefits of think-alouds became apparent to me when I was looking for ways to evaluate a new design for a gateway history course I was teaching in my college's program of general education. The new course design shifted emphasis from tidy summaries of historical knowledge delivered through lectures and textbooks toward activities and routines that uncovered the central questions, concepts, competencies, heuristics, and attitudes that characterize history as a disciplined way of thinking. In the new course, I introduced a new concept or competency related to historical thinking every week. I expected students to apply what they were learning to a series of iterative, identical essay assignments spaced at intervals throughout the course. This allowed me to measure student learning by comparing student performance on the essays generated by the first and last assignments. After several years of teaching the new course, the assessment results were disheartening. It was the rare student who showed steady progress at historical thinking from week to week. Remarkably, only a handful of the final essays were superior to the first ones. On the basis of this evidence, it seemed the new course design was a failure. I pouted a while, then wondered, Why aren't they learning? *What are they thinking?*

Prevost and Lemons (2016) used an innovative written think-aloud to explore what is going on in students' heads when they confront the most common form of assessment in college biology classrooms: multiple-choice problems about biology concepts. The article admirably demonstrated the potential of think-alouds for deepening theoretical knowledge of learning and innovating practical teaching strategies that improve learning.

It isn't easy to know what is going on in the minds of students. In my new course, I relied on close reading of student essays (see chapter 11), which generated the disappointing finding that they were not learning much. But I also used other ways to make students' thinking visible. The odd thing was that on course evaluations and self-reports, students who had completed the new course insisted they had learned a great deal. I was inclined to believe them as by the end of the term most of the students looked and sounded more intelligent. I was acting like an English public school inspector who after listening to student recitations rose and declared, "I have not been able to hear anything you have said, but I perceive by the intelligent look on your faces that you have fully mastered the text." Indubitably. Visual reconnaissance is a time-honored tool used to assess whether students are getting it. But time and experience show it is not to be trusted. Puzzled by the conflicting signals, I took advice from a colleague and turned to think-alouds to help me make sense of what was going on in my new course.

Think-alouds offer a window into thinking unmatched by other methodologies. For example, close reading of student writing is an essential tool for investigating what students know; it is a method I rely on to evaluate and grade student performances. But reading the final products of student work offers little help for figuring out why students recorded a wrong answer, retained certain misconceptions, or struggled unsuccessfully with an assignment. Writing researchers Hayes and Flower (1980), pioneers in using think-alouds to study student learning, compare analyzing the transcriptions generated by think-alouds (or protocols as researchers call them) to watching a dolphin break the surface of the sea. The dolphin's brief leaps through the air are like the glimpses provided by think-aloud protocols into the otherwise hidden mental processes of a learner:

> Between surfacings, the mental process, like the porpoise, runs deep and silent. Our task is to infer the course of the process from these brief traces. The power of protocol analysis lies in the richness of its data. Even though protocols are typically incomplete, they provide us with much more information about processes by which tasks are performed than does simply examining the outcome of the process. Knowing what answer people get in solving problems is much less informative than catching even fragmentary glimpses of the complex processes by which they arrive at the answer. (Hayes & Flower, 1980, pp. 9–10)

In the case of my new history course, close reading of the students' essays indicated they were not learning nearly as much as I wanted them to. But reading their papers could not tell me what the precise bottlenecks were, what dead-ends hemmed them in, or what external factors might be producing the disappointing results I saw.

Another difficulty with using written work to answer questions about thinking is the problem of validity. Because papers and other kinds of student-generated products rely on students' ability to articulate their thoughts in formal language, writing assignments conflate understanding with fluency. But sometimes the tongue-tied harbor deep understandings even though they write poorly. The reverse is true, as well; sometimes articulate students are able to say more than they really understand. This problem was first observed by Plato, who wrote an entire dialogue, *Meno*, to demonstrate the difference between knowledge and glib certainty. "The thorniest problem" (p. 79) of assessment, according to Wiggins and McTighe (1998), calls for differentiating between the quality of an insight and the quality of how the insight is expressed.

Of course I could have asked people to tell me what was going on inside their heads. And that I did, using course evaluations and a specially designed survey instrument to ask students what they thought they learned. The results of the survey revealed student perceptions about their learning, which were valuable to know. But it could not tell me whether and how much students actually did learn, and asking students to talk about their learning could not give me a front-row seat on their struggles to deploy the concepts and competencies I was teaching them. Asking students to talk about their thought processes after the fact creates problems that are familiar to historians— memories of witnesses can be false, recollection is always imperfect, and there is a natural human desire to narrate one's life as tidier, more linear, and more deliberate and purposeful than it actually was. Retrospection makes the process of understanding seem more orderly than it is, covering up the confusion, disorientation, mimicry of correct responses, and lucky guesses. The advantage of think-alouds is that they give us data gathered in real time as students struggle to formulate problem-solving strategies, employ skills, and develop insights.

At this point an alert reader might wonder that if it cannot be denied that people misremember and misreport even their recent past activities, why would one think that information provided about internal thought processes would be any more accurate? That is a good question, which left unanswered would cast doubt on the value of think-alouds as a research tool. But asking people about thought processes is not what happens in a think-aloud. The think-aloud technique asks people to report the contents of conscious cognition, not to make inferences about the processes used to arrive at these contents. People are encouraged to give online reports of everything that goes through their mind as they read a text or solve a problem. Typically, these reports are telegraphic, elliptical, filled with hunches and missteps, and are often difficult to interpret conclusively. They do, however, open a window to people's active construction of meaning and are useful despite their methodological shortcomings.

With these cautions in mind, how did I use think-alouds to study what was happening (and not happening) in my course? Of 60 students in the course, 12 were selected to participate in a think-aloud study, representing a cross-section of students in terms of gender, grade point average, and majors and nonmajors. For their participation, students were paid $10 an hour. In Week 1 of the course, my student research assistants and I sat down with each student individually in a room equipped with a tape recorder. We trained students to become proficient at thinking out loud, using an anagram exercise to make them comfortable verbalizing their thoughts, everything from the sublime to the ridiculous. This took about 10 to 15 minutes. Then we presented students with documents concerning the Battle of the Little Bighorn, a subject most knew little about. We asked our subjects to think out loud while making sense of the documents. This was essentially the same task they would perform 8 times over the length of the course, the difference being that in this case their thoughts would be unfiltered because they were not composing an essay. With the tape recorder running, subjects read through the documents aloud, verbalizing any and all thoughts that occurred to them. When subjects fell silent, we would prompt them to think out loud or to elaborate on their thoughts as they attempted to make sense of the historical evidence.

Our think-aloud sessions lasted anywhere from 40 to 90 minutes. After all 12 sessions were completed, the tape recordings were transcribed for analysis. Analysis took the form of coding each discrete verbalization in the transcript according to the type of thinking it exemplified. We identified 15 distinct types of thinking processes displayed in the protocols, from the uncategorizable ("It sure is hot in here") to comprehension monitoring ("I don't understand what he's saying here") to the types of historical thinking we were particularly looking for, such as sourcing a document ("I can't trust Whittaker, he wasn't there"), asking a historical question ("What really caused this battle?"), or recognizing limits to knowledge ("I need to see more evidence"). After coding each think-aloud independently, we used a rubric to rate each subject's proficiency on the 6 thinking skills taught in the course. The rubric's 5-point Likert scale ranged from 1, indicating the undeveloped ability of an average high school graduate, to 5, indicating a sophistication comparable to that of a professional historian. We then compared our coded transcripts until reaching consensus on how to rate the students' abilities in the 6 key areas. To prevent my bias as the course designer from influencing the results, we also contracted with an independent analyst to help us code the transcripts and rate students' abilities.

At the end of the term, the 12 subjects completed a second think-aloud on a different subject, the 1886 Haymarket Affair. When these sessions had been transcribed and coded and the subjects' abilities rated, we compared the first and second think-alouds to determine whether students made gains in historical thinking using the concepts and competencies I had set as outcomes for the course.

The results? Overall, the think-alouds revealed cognitive enhancements that were not as dramatic as what the students claimed for themselves in their glowing self-reports. But the gains were much greater than indicated by close readings of early and late papers. It came as a relief to know that although the course could benefit from modifications, there was no reason to scrap the new design altogether and go back to the drawing board to start over.

The best thing about the think-alouds, though, were the unanticipated insights I gained as I eavesdropped on students while they made sense of historical materials. For example, I learned that underperforming students struggle less with historical thinking than they do with reading itself. Moreover, in the second set of think-alouds, I noted that some of the best meaning-making came from students who in the gradebook were steady B and C performers. For them, deep understandings seemed to evaporate when they tried to wrestle their thoughts onto paper. This told me that I had work to do if I wanted to distinguish between assessing understanding and assessing students' ability to communicate their understanding. Thus, a pair of competencies I had given little thought to—reading comprehension and prose writing—were shown by the think-alouds to be sizable roadblocks to demonstrating historical thinking. This finding led to changes in the course such as shorter reading assignments and new interventions to assist with writing.

In the course of running the think-alouds, I also learned why student performances on the final essay were so disappointing. Several students mentioned how tired and overworked they were by the end of the term, preventing them from giving their best effort to final assignments. When I altered the design of the course to allow students to nominate one of their last three essays as an example of their best work, performance on that essay showed improvement over the first essay by an average of one and a half grade levels. I could live with that.

Meanwhile, brain lint happens. In 2009 when instructors at several California community colleges formed an action research project to improve pedagogical practice and enhance student learning, they spent time watching and discussing videotapes of think-alouds in which students read text and attempted to solve pre-algebra problems. The exercise proved transformative. The teachers were amazed by the misconceptions escaping their detection. Students making progress in their grade books were observed to repeatedly misuse even simple procedures; basic knowledge and problem-solving skills the instructors took for granted as natural were often missing. Bond (2009), a leading American researcher in educational and psychological measurement, summarizes their (and my) experience with think-alouds this way:

> Indeed, the richness and depth of insight into student thinking that the "think-aloud" technique affords faculty cannot be overstated. Only by finding out what students are and are not learning can instructors effectively redesign their instruction or course. This is assessment at its most informative. (p. 10)

References

Barzun, J. (1945). *Teacher in America*. Boston, MA: Little, Brown.

Bond, L. (2009). *Toward informative assessment and a culture of evidence: Results from strengthening pre-collegiate education in community colleges (SPECC)*. Stanford, CA: Carnegie Foundation for the Advancement of Teaching.

Calder, L. (2006). Uncoverage: Toward a signature pedagogy for the history survey. *Journal of American History, 92*, 1358–1370.

Hayes, J., & Flower, L. (1980). Identifying the organization of writing processes. In L. W. Gregg & E. R. Steinberg (Eds.), *Cognitive processes in writing* (pp. 3–30). Hillsdale, NJ: Erlbaum.

Prevost, L. B., & Lemons, P. P. (2016). Step by step: Biology undergraduates' problem-solving procedures during multiple-choice assessment. *CBE Life–Sciences Education, 15*(4), Article 71. doi:10.1187/cbe.15-12-0255

Steiner, G. (2005). *Lessons of the masters* (Rev. ed.). Cambridge, MA: Harvard University Press.

Wiggins, G., & McTighe, J. (1998). *Understanding by design*. Alexandria, VA: Association for Supervision and Curriculum Development.

Wineburg, S. S. (1991). On the reading of historical texts: Notes on the breach between school and academy. *American Educational Research Journal, 28*, 495–519.

PART THREE

MAKING AN IMPACT

13

WRITING SoTL

Going Public for an Extended Audience

Jessie L. Moore

Since 2006 I have spent four days in late May and early June cofacilitating an annual scholarship of teaching and learning (SoTL) writing residency for Elon University faculty. Although the dedicated time to write and structured opportunities for feedback on work-in-progress routinely attract veteran SoTL scholars, each year also brings faculty who are writing for a SoTL audience for the first time. In this chapter, I explore lessons learned about writing SoTL, from my own writing and from facilitating the SoTL writing residency.

Writing is an important part of SoTL. As Felten (2013) contends,

> Because SoTL inquiry typically is iterative and highly contextual, the most appropriate ways to go public should capture and reflect the evolving nature of this form of research. . . . Regardless of the format, however, good practice in SoTL requires that both the process and the products of inquiry are public so that colleagues can critique and use the work. (pp. 123–124)

McKinney (2007) reminds us there are multiple ways to go public with SoTL, and expectations are socially constructed, so they may change over time. Depending on our career stage or institutional reward structures, we also may experience differences in how various ways of making SoTL work public are valued. Given that, McKinney suggests going public with SoTL in sequential steps, perhaps first with a course or teaching portfolio, then a conference presentation, and finally a publication. In my own experience reviewing portfolios for promotion and tenure decisions, this type of ongoing and evolving public pathway often demonstrates a sustained commitment to a SoTL question, enabling scholars to discuss how their research has progressed and how they have used early feedback to shape continued work on a project. Of course we need to be attentive to our institution's promotion criteria and strategic about how our target publications and comprehensive scholarly profile align with institutional values. (See McKinney, 2007, for additional tips about documenting SoTL work for tenure and promotion.) Once we make a commitment to writing SoTL, though, the following strategies and practices may increase our scholarly productivity and the likelihood of others engaging with our texts.

Who Is My Audience?

For many new SoTL writers, adjusting to a SoTL audience presents a significant hurdle. As academics, we have years of practice writing for members of our own field; we are familiar with disciplinary norms for constructing and supporting arguments, integrating prior scholarship, and editing for sentence-level stylistic choices. We have less experience writing for multidisciplinary audiences.

When I am writing SoTL, I identify a journal or other publication as a possible venue before I spend too much time drafting, and I encourage my colleagues who participate in the SoTL writing residency to do the same. Selecting a specific publication opens up strategies for learning more about my SoTL audience. If I choose a multidisciplinary journal, such as *Teaching & Learning Inquiry* or *College Teaching*, I know I will need to be attentive to defining and explaining any terms or concepts that might be unique to my discipline or that might have a differently nuanced meaning in another field. If I choose a disciplinary SoTL publication like *Research in the Teaching of English* or *Teaching Philosophy* or *Teaching Mathematics and Its Applications*, I know I can use disciplinary terms, and although I still may need to explain how they inform my specific project, I likely won't need to define them as much. (See University of Central Florida Faculty Center for Teaching and Learning, 2010, for a list of journals on teaching and learning.)

Once I have chosen a possible publication venue, I review that publication for prior literature related to my topic. Ideally, SoTL researchers conduct a literature review during the design phase of a project so the research design is responsive to prior work (see chapter 3), but revisiting or expanding our review of the existing scholarship when we are writing SoTL can help us identify new publications we may have overlooked earlier. Looking at other articles in our target publication also gives us an opportunity to examine the recurring characteristics of articles in the journal such as the types of supporting evidence used, organizational structures that seem common across articles, citation styles, and other discourse conventions specific to the journal.

In addition to considering whether terminology is discipline specific and analyzing genre conventions, SoTL writers need to consider if our word choices transcend geographic boundaries. For example, the people we call *faculty* in some regions are referred to as *academic staff* in others. Concepts also may resonate differently; in the United States, for instance, we discuss high-impact practices (Kuh, 2008), but those words carry another significance beyond the realm of U.S.-based higher education research, as Sutherland (2015), a New Zealand scholar, reminds us when she suggests

> Enhancement and effectiveness give us already two other
> words to counter the
> Violence of
> Impact.
> Such a slamming, crashing, thudding
> word that bumps against and
> into our disciplinary colleagues. (p. 109)

Intentionally extending our literature reviews to include international journals and publications from other regions helps SoTL writers make meaningful language choices that also engage a broader audience.

What Is My Purpose?

The rhetorical moves of considering audience and purpose are not unique to writing SoTL, but SoTL may offer new purposes for our writing. For instance, although we often conduct scholarship to advance disciplinary knowledge, we might share SoTL results to inform future teaching practices. Alternatively, we might demonstrate that a pedagogy previously considered context specific is generalizable to other institution types or learning situations. We even might seek to inform education policy. In some cases, our findings may not add significantly to teaching and learning conversations, but our research *methods* offer a new way to explore an inquiry question, so our purpose for writing focuses on the *how*, the process of inquiry, rather than on the outcomes.

Thinking about the intersection of our target audience and our intended purpose can guide other writing choices. For instance, if we want to inform education policy, we might include case studies from our data, highlighting

Psychologists Bernstein and Greenhoot (2014) demonstrated how SoTL writers can represent data and concepts in multiple formats. In addition to explaining their data and analysis in text, they provided visual representations in tables and figures, including data charts and process maps.

the potential impact of a specific practice for real people (e.g., our participants). If we opt to share a new research strategy, we might include more visual representations of our research time line and step-by-step practices. If we are trying to make a complex research finding accessible to our international, multidisciplinary audience, we might present our results in multiple ways, such as written text, tables, and figures.

What Do I Bring to the Conversation?

Even though my colleagues who are new to writing SoTL might be familiar with considering their audience and purpose, writing for a new-to-them audience and purpose may invoke doubts about what they can contribute to the conversation. If we are writing SoTL, we inherently bring an interest in teaching and learning in exploring new or revised teaching practices to support our students' learning, and our readers share those values. If we take the time to adjust our word choices and stylistic conventions to connect with an international, multidisciplinary audience, we typically will encounter engaged colleagues who are eager to learn with us to enhance classroom (and beyond the classroom) teaching, support student learning, and inform education policy at our institutions and beyond.

Manarin (2016) offered an example of writing SoTL that is grounded in the arts and humanities, specifically sharing results from close reading strategies typical of textual analysis with attentiveness to both textual and visual elements. All issues of the journal Teaching & Learning Inquiry *are available online for free, so new scholars can find examples with other disciplinary perspectives by browsing the issues.*

We each also bring our unique disciplinary practices and perspectives to writing SoTL, and our disciplinary lenses enrich SoTL conversations by lending a wider mix of theoretical frames and research methods to our shared work. For instance, a biologist may bring a commitment to research designs with comparison groups, a political scientist may bring strategies for large-scale survey research, and a historian may bring strategies for close readings of student work. Collectively, these varied research methods contribute to a more nuanced understanding of student learning, helping us understand effectiveness across student identity groups or institutional contexts and providing a deep dive into the enhancement of learning for specific students. The potential power of these mixed methods increases when we describe our research practices using terms that are accessible to a broad cross-section of colleagues, so identifying a group of multidisciplinary critical friends (e.g., Baskerville & Goldblatt, 2009) to read drafts of our methods and other sections of our writing helps raise our own awareness of discipline-specific practices we may need to explain for our SoTL readers.

In addition to providing a range of examples of student-faculty partnerships in SoTL, each chapter in Werder and Otis (2009) is coauthored with students, illustrating a range of strategies for writing SoTL collaboratively. Some chapters have a dialogue structure to represent student and faculty voices; others use quotes from the individual coauthors; and others model a unified, collaborative voice.

Feedback and Accountability From Critical Friends

As my colleagues and I note in descriptions of our campus's SoTL writing residency, dedicated time and space, frequent feedback, peer pressure to write, and friendly support for setting and meeting goals can help scholars advance a writing project (Felten, Moore, & Strickland, 2009; Moore, Felten, & Strickland, 2013). Although individual writers may not be able to replicate all features of a writing retreat, writing groups can provide three of these elements: frequent feedback, peer pressure to write, and assistance with setting goals. My own writing group typically meets twice a month, and we each share a draft a few days ahead of our meeting. Often we don't share complete drafts, but we commit to sharing chunks, such as an outline or a literature review, a methods description, or a discussion section, so that we maintain forward progress on our writing no matter how hectic our lives feel. Receiving timely feedback helps us move past the potential stumbling block of wondering if anyone will be interested in our writing; we know how readers are reacting to our work in progress, so we are less hesitant about continuing to write. Sword (2012) suggests writing with "at least *five real people*" in mind, including "a top expert in your field . . . , a close colleague in your discipline . . . , an academic colleague from outside your discipline, an advanced undergraduate in your discipline, [and] a nonacademic friend, relative, or neighbor" (p. 46, emphasis in original). Our writing group takes this strategy a step further by actually sharing our writing with at least a few of these authentic readers who help us make sense of where we need to clarify a concept, extend a description, or more explicitly connect evidence to our argument. Significantly, our group members are critical friends, trusted colleagues who offer thoughtful critiques but also root for our success (Baskerville & Goldblatt, 2009; Costa & Kallick, 1993); therefore, we find it easier to grapple with our group's feedback because we know we are trying to help each other write more effective texts.

In addition to providing just-in-time feedback, my writing group replicates the goal setting and accountability features of the writing residency. At the end of meetings, each member shares a writing goal for the next session, and group members help us gauge the feasibility of those goals. I tend to set overly ambitious goals, and my colleagues help rein in my expectations to more manageable chunks so that I'm not disappointed by limited progress. We challenge another colleague to share work in progress, even if she thinks it's not polished enough for outside readers so that she continues to advance her scholarly agenda as she adjusts to her faculty role, and we share strategies for making time to write amid teaching, course preparations, and committee service. A third colleague has a tendency to procrastinate by reading more and more related literature, so we frequently encourage her to write a few sentences connecting what she's reading to her project. Frequent writing group meetings typically promote more frequent writing as writing group members provide accountability for regular writing to support individual members' goals and to respect group members' time (Fajt et al., 2013). We want to see each other succeed, and we value the feedback we receive from this network of readers.

Maintaining Momentum

Writing SoTL remains work, though. Granted, it's fun and rewarding work, but it requires a commitment to keep writing, particularly when our professional lives pull us in multiple directions. (While writing this paragraph, I've been interrupted several times to address time-sensitive questions about a service commitment!) Strategies we use for all our professional writing can help us advance our SoTL writing. As an early writing step, I typically draft and revise an informal outline for my project with potential headings, notes to myself, and quotes or concepts I want to integrate from prior scholarship so that I can identify smaller chunks to work on as my schedule allows. This strategy allows me to make progress on a project, even if I only have

30 minutes to devote to a paragraph or so. I don't have to wait until I have hours of uninterrupted time because I'm making visible to my future self where I can jump back into my SoTL writing for whatever time I have on a given day.

When I need to step away from my writing to turn my attention to other commitments, I take a few minutes to make notes about where I might pick up when I come back to it. For the current section in this chapter, my note reads, "Other tips—Stop at a point when you can start again. Be open to 'parking' ideas and to one article becoming more than one." If I hadn't included this note as an example, no one but me would have read this informal note, and it jogged my memory about two strategies I wanted to share next. For some SoTL writers, stopping at a point when or where they can start again means giving themselves low-hanging fruit for the beginning of their next writing session; if I procrastinate about writing (which I admittedly do), starting a writing session by turning a detailed outline into a paragraph can provide needed motivation to begin—and keep—writing. The sense of accomplishment becomes a springboard for writing the next part of the draft.

As my example note to myself previews, a final strategy is to be receptive to setting tangential ideas aside for future articles or dividing a particularly complex draft into multiple pieces. I routinely keep a separate file open when I'm writing so I can copy and paste snippets into it for future writing projects. Perhaps writing about my current project sparked an idea that I needed to write down so that I can turn my attention back to the task at hand; I'm not discarding or discounting the idea, but I am giving myself permission to capture the idea and come back to it later. Sometimes our SoTL projects are so complex that even though we only anticipated writing one article we need more space to discuss the details and their significance for teaching and learning. Being open to splitting a project into multiple articles may give us the flexibility to describe each subtopic in ways that will better resonate with our international, multi-institutional audiences. Plus, multiple articles stemming from a research project may help us demonstrate a sustained, scholarly trajectory to supervisors and promotions and tenure committees.

Ultimately, writing SoTL is a key component of SoTL; writing SoTL means going public with our teaching and learning inquiry in a medium that transcends time and space. SoTL conferences (see chapter 16) provide a space to share early analyses of findings, get feedback on work in progress, and engage in conversations with others who are thinking about teaching and learning. Writing SoTL takes those conversations a step further by sharing our work with an audience that extends beyond our institutions, beyond the subset of SoTL scholars able to attend a conference, and potentially beyond disciplinary and geographic boundaries. Done well, writing SoTL puts our work in conversation with prior scholarship and opens up portals for others to respond to our research, add to it, and continue the dialogue for years to come.

References

Baskerville, D., & Goldblatt, H. (2009). Learning to be a critical friend: From professional indifference through challenge to unguarded conversations. *Cambridge Journal of Education, 39*, 205–221.

Bernstein, D., & Greenhoot, A. F. (2014). Team-designed improvement of writing and critical thinking in large undergraduate courses. *Teaching & Learning Inquiry, 2*(1). Retrieved from http://tlijournal.com/tli/index.php/TLI/article/view/72/68

Costa, A. L., & Kallick, B. (1993). Through the lens of a critical friend. *Educational Leadership, 51*(2), 49–51.

Fajt, V., Gelwick, F. I., Loureiro-Rodríguez, V., Merton, P., Moore, G., Moyna, M. I., & Zarestky, J. (2013). Feedback and fellowship: Stories from a successful writing group. In A. E. Geller & M. Eodice (Eds.), *Working with faculty writers* (pp. 163–174). Boulder, CO: University Press of Colorado.

Felten, P. (2013). Principles of good practice in SoTL. *Teaching & Learning Inquiry, 1*(1), 121–125. Retrieved from http://tlijournal.com/tli/index.php/TLI/article/view/39/14

Felten, P., Moore, J. L., & Strickland, M. (2009). Faculty writing residencies: Supporting scholarly writing and teaching. *Journal on Centers for Teaching and Learning, 1*, 39–55.

Kuh, G. D. (2008). *High-impact educational practices: What they are, who has access to them, and why they matter.* Washington DC: Association of American Colleges & Universities.

Manarin, K. (2016). Interpreting undergraduate research posters in the literature classroom. *Teaching & Learning Inquiry, 4*(1). Retrieved from http://tlijournal.com/tli/index.php/TLI/article/view/128/80

McKinney, K. (2007). *Enhancing learning through the scholarship of teaching and learning: The challenges and joys of juggling.* San Francisco, CA: Anker.

Moore, J. L., Felten, P., & Strickland, M. (2013). Supporting a culture of writing: Faculty writing residences as a WAC initiative. In A. E. Geller & M. Eodice (Eds.), *Working with faculty writers* (pp. 127–141). Boulder, CO: University Press of Colorado.

Sutherland, K. (2015). Language. *Teaching & Learning Inquiry, 3*, 109–110.

Sword, H. (2012). *Stylish academic writing.* Cambridge, MA: Harvard University Press.

University of Central Florida Faculty Center for Teaching and Learning. (2010). *SoTL journals.* Retrieved from http://www.fctl.ucf.edu/researchandscholarship/sotl/journals/index.php

Werder, C., & Otis, M. M. (Eds.). (2009). *Engaging student voices in the study of teaching and learning.* Sterling, VA: Stylus.

14

READING SoTL

Exploring Scholarly Conversations

David J. Voelker

Reading the scholarship of teaching and learning (SoTL) is a powerful way to partake in the teaching commons (Huber & Hutchings, 2005). SoTL allows higher educators to look behind the previously closed classroom doors of our colleagues, granting us access to not only the experiences of other teachers and students but also evidence of learning that has been systematically collected and analyzed. This research into student learning carried out by teaching practitioners has the virtue of bringing diverse perspectives and methods to bear on the complex problem of learning in a higher education context. Reading SoTL, though, can be challenging or even frustrating, precisely because of this diversity of context, discipline, and methodology. Exploring SoTL literature often takes us out of our own fields of academic expertise, which can mean wading through unfamiliar tables of data or navigating a free-flowing essay with many twists and turns. Reading SoTL often requires translation as we convert insights and meanings from one discipline or context into another. Often the translation is relatively straightforward; in some cases it may be more like translating free verse than translating utilitarian phrases such as "Which way to the library?" Approaching this literature flexibly but with a clear sense of purpose and a well-defined reading strategy, however, makes reading SoTL manageable and well worth the effort.

Why Read SoTL?

An academic who lacks familiarity with SoTL might assume that the only reason to read SoTL is to obtain ideas for specific techniques for improving learning. Indeed, many SoTL publications focus on What works? kinds

Staudinger (2017) offered an especially insightful example of a study that evaluated strategies for helping students complete reading assignments and prepare to participate in discussions.

of questions (Hutchings, 2000), and the SoTL literature is brimming over with helpful suggestions for teaching techniques and assignments.

Although there is much to learn from reading focused studies of student learning, there are other compelling reasons to read SoTL. In addition to providing us with a better understanding of how to cultivate learning, SoTL can also give insight into how we define *learning* and how we evaluate or assess learning, whether for the purposes of grading or research. SoTL devotes plenty of attention to the fine details of teaching, examining specific techniques, assignments, and activities, but it also takes into account larger issues such as course design and learning outcomes.

Many SoTL studies examine the effectiveness of particular approaches to teaching. I have found that any time I am considering implementing a new approach in my own classes, it is worth the investment of time to find out what other instructors have discovered and documented regarding similar approaches. For example, a biology instructor revamping an introductory biology course to increase the student success rate while maintaining rigor would be well served to explore the extensive SoTL work on this topic.

My examples suggest that we might read SoTL to help us think about how to cultivate learning, evaluate learning, and collaborate to design courses and curricula. In many fields SoTL has delved even deeper to explore the foundations of knowledge and how to define *learning* at the introductory, advanced, and graduate levels. In my own discipline of history, for example, SoTL scholars have engaged in a lively debate over the desired learning outcomes for undergraduate students. Publications by educational psychologist

Freeman, Haak, and Wenderoth (2011) allow readers to quickly get an idea of how effective such interventions as clicker questions, reading quizzes, and practice exams might be for helping students learn and succeed, based on their experience revamping an introductory biology course.

Wineburg (2001) and historian Calder (2006), for example, have deepened the conversation among historians about teaching and learning and have moved them in new directions. Wineburg's insights into the ways historical thinking is "unnatural" (p. 3; i.e., not intuitive and automatic), along with Calder's critique of the "coverage model" (p. 1359) of teaching history at the introductory level, have changed the field. Expanding on this work, Sipress and Voelker (2008, 2011) have made a case that historical argumentation (rather than content coverage) should be the organizing principle for introductory history courses, whereas Calder (2013) has proposed that narrative would be a more fruitful approach. Inspired at least in part by the new SoTL in history, the American Historical Association (2017) spent several years developing a history discipline core and creating a list of core competencies and learning outcomes, which focuses not on content knowledge but on how history students understand what it means to think historically, do historical research, and apply historical knowledge. This ongoing dialogue among history educators could provide a model for other disciplines for how to examine long-standing pedagogical practices in light of new research on learning. Reading SoTL in history, one can observe and learn from an evolving, research-based conversation about student learning and the very nature of learning in this field. Similar conversations have been underway in many other disciplines. Tapping into this literature through SoTL has become a critical way of understanding what it means to teach and practice in the disciplines.

Bernstein and Greenhoot (2014) described and evaluated a team-based approach to developing critical thinking in large-enrollment classes. As is the case with many good SoTL articles, this study went well beyond enumerating a list of discrete teaching strategies. In addition to exploring specific pedagogical interventions, this article addressed another set of key SoTL issues, specifically, how we evaluate student learning. Notably, the article went further still by describing and evaluating a team-based course design strategy involving librarians, writing center staff, and graduate fellows, illustrating that SoTL can have expansive implications for not only classroom learning but also intra-institutional collaborations. Although their study focused on introductory social science courses, their framework of cognitive-apprenticeship framework, assessment strategies, and team-based approach could be applied to large-enrollment introductory courses in just about any discipline.

Such conversations, however, have not simply been contained in the disciplines. Teaching and learning are clearly interdisciplinary activities, so SoTL has often made collaborators of instructors and scholars from various disciplines. Reading SoTL from various disciplines provides a powerful way of improving learning and research into learning in one's own discipline. In my view, some of the most valuable SoTL books have been edited collections based on cross-disciplinary collaborations, including Chick, Haynie, and Gurung (2012); Gurung, Chick, and Haynie (2009); and Pace and Middendorf (2004). Additionally, the authors in McKinney (2013) engage in a rich discussion of the challenges and benefits of a multidisciplinary or interdisciplinary approach to studying student learning. These books should be considered essential reading for any budding SoTL scholar. In the inter-disciplinary "trading zone" of SoTL (Huber & Morreale, 2002, p. 3), there is much to be learned about not only methods for doing pedagogical research but also definitions and the cultivation of learning in the different corners of the academy. Reading SoTL and having conversations across the disciplines can help break down the walls that usually divide higher educators.

When reading SoTL, it is a good idea to be flexible. We should bring different expectations from those we bring to reviewing an article for publi-cation in a top-tier journal or reviewing a tenure file. Reading SoTL publica-tions can be quite useful for our teaching practice, even if it doesn't resemble what we count as original and rigorous research in our particular discipline. For example, I adapted an ecological mapping exercise (Hill, Wilson, & Watson, 2004) based on a large body of research in transformative education, even though the article is not grounded in what historians would consider evidence of student learning. Moreover, I can now use evolving ecological maps as evidence of my own students' learning by comparing maps from the beginning of the semester with end-of-semester maps.

Strategies for Purposeful Reading

Although there are important books on SoTL and pedagogical research, most articles on SoTL are available online. Given that there are now scores of SoTL journals and hundreds of articles published each year, it can be easy for SoTL newcomers to be overwhelmed. (See chapter 3 for help finding useful research.) To manage this challenge, I suggest using a strategy for pur-poseful reading by having specific questions in mind, using efficient reading practices, and managing the materials and notes in an organized fashion. In other words, we can read SoTL using strategies similar to those we use for reading disciplinary research.

When getting started exploring a new SoTL topic, it makes sense to begin with what's new in the field. For example, if I'm interested in learning more about how students wrestle with threshold concepts, I could start by reading several articles, regardless of discipline, that explore learning through this lens. Scholarship, say, from the past five years is likely to be based on well-defined and well-developed concepts. That said, I should also keep an eye out for citations that recur in multiple publications. In other words, in addition to looking for what's new, it is important to also pay attention to what's enduring. Some databases even allow researchers to locate other articles that cite the foundational articles. In the case of threshold concepts, for example, I'll need to read the foundational piece by Meyer and Land (2003), as well as later studies relevant to my own field.

In addition to getting to know the state of the field, I can also read strategically by having a few specific questions in mind. Imagine that for the coming semester I want to do more to help my students become better readers. I'd quickly find a vast literature on reading and teaching advanced literacy at the college level. (Here is a good chance to practice placing some boundaries on reading by finding several recent publications and a few enduring classics.) After I've scratched the surface of this vexing problem of reading, I'd likely want to focus my inquiry. In the course I have in mind, students seem to struggle with reading online, so I can start looking for research in a more focused way. I'd then come across the Association of College and Research Libraries' (2016) framework for information literacy, which uses threshold concepts to define *online literacy* and includes a helpful biography of some of the most influential scholarship for my refocused topic of online literacy.

In addition to reading with problem-focused questions in mind, as noted previously, it can be helpful to think critically about how we can translate any SoTL publication into the language of our own courses, disciplines, or SoTL research. Key questions to ask include the following:

- What did these researchers learn about student learning? (Note that sometimes they learn something quite different from what they set out to learn.)
- What is the context of the learning discussed in this study? (Who were the students, what forms did their learning take, etc.?)
- How does this context relate to the context of my own classes and my specific students?
- How might I adapt and apply the insights of this study to my context?

Because SoTL scholars often read articles outside their immediate fields, it may be difficult to determine in advance how useful an article might be. Reading abstracts before downloading can help, but I recommend downloading articles in batches of at least several articles at a time. When I review the files, I can quickly delete any articles that do not seem useful, and when I find an article to retain, I rename the file to make it easier to locate in the future (e.g., the author's last name, a shortened version of the title, and the year of publication, such as Brayboy-Tribal Critical Race Theory-2006.pdf). We can also make annotations or take notes on articles the first time we read them. Depending on our purpose for reading, it might suffice simply to make some brief notes to assist our course design. If we're conducting a literature review, of course, we may need more detailed notes, such as a brief description of the research question and findings of the study. Additionally, if we're compiling a bibliography, we can make a list of other sources to consult later.

A key observation for SoTL reading is that the goal of efficiency may not always serve us well. Although articles written following the introduction, methods, results, and discussion style can be read quickly, essay-style articles usually require more time, at least until we find something that directly concerns our own teaching or research concerns. Although reading an open-ended essay takes patience, this format can allow a complex and multilayered analysis of a teaching and learning problem.

Conclusion

In addition to being essential for conducting pedagogical research, reading SoTL is a powerful way to engage in scholarly or critical teaching. Given the many pressures on higher educators, it's fair to ask, Who has the time? Perhaps finding or making time is the most difficult thing about reading SoTL. If we claim to take a scholarly approach to evaluating and documenting our students' learning, we need to touch base with SoTL on a regular basis. But what about those of us who are not interested or able to pursue a scholarly agenda focused on teaching and learning? There are other relatively easy ways to benefit from SoTL. *Teaching & Learning Inquiry* and the *International Journal for the Scholarship of Teaching and Learning* are open-access publications available online. We could make a practice of spending one to two hours per month, or even per quarter, skimming and reading these journals or other relevant disciplinary teaching and learning journals. Even one hour per month could be useful. Another option is to follow SoTL journals or scholars on social media. A good place to start is to follow an organization like the International Society for the Scholarship of Teaching and Learning (@ISSOTL) on Twitter and pay attention to whom and what they are retweeting. From there, one can find relevant scholars to follow on Twitter. For those who avoid social media, another option is to join or form a campus SoTL reading group. Many higher educators are eager to discuss teaching with colleagues but seldom have the time or space; a monthly reading group can be an excellent remedy.

The important thing, I think, is to find some way to take advantage of the teaching and learning commons that has emerged and expanded with the rise of SoTL. Not every higher educator has the time or resources to conduct SoTL research, but as professional practitioners, we should be dedicated to continuously improving our craft, and reading SoTL is an essential tool for supporting this ongoing process.

References

American Historical Association. (2017). *Tuning the history discipline in the United States.* Retrieved from https://www.historians.org/teaching-and-learning/tuning/history-discipline-core

Association of College and Research Libraries. (2016). *Framework for information literacy for higher education.* Retrieved from http://www.ala.org/acrl/standards/ilframework

Bernstein, D., & Greenhoot, A. F. (2014). Team-designed improvement of writing and critical thinking in large undergraduate courses. *Teaching & Learning Inquiry, 2*(1), 39–61.

Calder, L. (2006). Uncoverage: Toward a signature pedagogy for the history survey. *Journal of American History, 92,* 1358–1370.

Calder, L. (2013). The stories we tell. *OAH Magazine of History, 27*(3), 5–8.

Chick, N. L., Haynie, A., & Gurung, R. A. R. (Eds.). (2012). *Exploring more signature pedagogies: Approaches to teaching disciplinary habits of mind.* Sterling, VA: Stylus.

Freeman, S., Haak, D., & Wenderoth, M. P. (2011). Increased course structure improves performance in introductory biology. *CBE–Life Sciences Education, 10,* 175–186.

Gurung, R. A. R., Chick, N. L., & Haynie, A. (Eds.). (2009). *Exploring signature pedagogies: Approaches to teaching disciplinary habits of mind.* Sterling, VA: Stylus.

Hill, S. B., Wilson, S., & Watson, K. (2004). Learning ecology. In E. O'Sullivan & M. M. Taylor (Eds.), *Learning toward an ecological consciousness: Selected transformative practices* (pp. 47–84). New York, NY: Palgrave Macmillan.

Huber, M. T., & Hutchings, P. (2005). *The advancement of learning: Building the teaching commons.* San Francisco, CA: Jossey-Bass.

Huber, M. T., & Morreale, S. P. (2002). Situating the scholarship of teaching and learning: A cross-disciplinary conversation. In M. T. Huber & S. P. Morreale (Eds.), *Disciplinary styles in the scholarship of teaching and learning: Exploring common ground* (pp. 1–24). Washington DC: American Association for Higher Education and the Carnegie Foundation for the Advancement of Teaching.

Hutchings, P. (2000). Approaching the scholarship of teaching and learning. In P. Hutchings (Ed.), *Opening lines: Approaches to the scholarship of teaching and learning* (pp. 4–6). Menlo Park, CA: Carnegie Foundation for the Advancement of Teaching.

McKinney, K. (Ed.). (2013). *The scholarship of teaching and learning in and across the disciplines.* Bloomington, IN: Indiana University Press.

Meyer, J., & Land, R. (2003). *Threshold concepts and troublesome knowledge: Linkages to ways of thinking and practising within the disciplines.* Retrieved from http://www.etl.tla.ed.ac.uk/docs/ETLreport4.pdf

Pace, D., & Middendorf, J. K. (Eds.). (2004). *Decoding the disciplines: Helping students learn disciplinary ways of thinking.* San Francisco, CA: Jossey-Bass.

Sipress, J. M., & Voelker, D. J. (2008). From learning history to doing history: Beyond the coverage model. In R. A. R. Gurung, N. L. Chick, & A. Haynie (Eds.), *Exploring signature pedagogies: Approaches to teaching disciplinary habits of mind* (pp. 19–35). Sterling, VA: Stylus.

Sipress, J. M., & Voelker, D. J. (2011). The end of the history survey course: The rise and fall of the coverage model. *Journal of American History, 97,* 1050–1066.

Staudinger, A. K. (2017). Reading deeply for disciplinary awareness and political judgment. *Teaching & Learning Inquiry, 5*(1), 1–16.

Wineburg, S. S. (2001). *Historical thinking and other unnatural acts: Charting the future of teaching the past.* Philadelphia, PA: Temple University Press.

15

DEVELOPING SoTL LOCALLY

From Classroom to Learning Object

Dan Bernstein

L ike many instructors, I have always reflected on how well students are doing in my classes, and I try to improve the depth of their understanding each time I offer a course. I have also worked to increase the percentage of students who demonstrate understanding at the highest levels of sophistication. I suppose I have been a little different from some in that I consider students' work on assignments to be my guide for improvement rather than using their perceptions of my courses as the primary driver for change. I do carefully consider students' perceptions to understand their experience of the learning environment I have constructed, but that is not a substitute for close reading of their intellectual work on the assignments I provide.

My efforts in this regard were largely informal and ad hoc until I was invited to join a small community of colleagues convened by the Carnegie Foundation for the Advancement of Teaching in 1998. During a summer gathering of the cohort, we were invited to identify a specific question to explore in a single course the following year. I was quite taken by several conversations I had with a Carnegie scholar named Tom Hatch (now on the education faculty at Columbia University), and his questions and challenges gave me a clear focus for my project. I was proud of the fact that in 20 years of college teaching I had never once given a multiple-choice test, even when teaching very large courses. I displayed the conceptual essay prompts that I used for exams, and I was able to describe in some detail how well students did on those exam questions. I could even identify which parts of the complex questions were best (and worst) understood.

Hatch had worked with Project Zero in Boston, and he pointed me to an edited volume of work derived from that project (*Teaching for Understanding:*

135

Linking Research With Practice, edited by Martha Stone Wiske [1997]). Based on their work defining *understanding,* he asked me if I thought that my students could use the conceptual frameworks they developed to solve specific problems related to those analyses. Being a late-onset Bloom's taxonomy kind of guy, I argued that conceptual understanding was a higher order skill than application, so of course they could do the simpler task. Hatch double-dog dared me to evaluate that claim with evidence, and I had a year's work nicely laid out for me. I decided to take one of my undergraduate courses and transform all the exams from conceptual prompts to vignette-based word problems in which students would use the conceptual material to analyze the specific cases described.

This little exercise was more than a little disruptive as I had the target course very well refined, and this meant developing entirely new examinations. I had three midterm exams and a final exam, and all the midterms could be taken a second time (on an alternate form). With four of these essays on each exam, it was a lot of new development to be done. One important part of the Project Zero definition of *understanding* is that someone who deeply understands can use the idea in ways and in contexts the instructor had not explicitly taught (Wiske, 1997). Others call this *transfer* or *generalization,* but I agreed that my use of conceptual exam prompts implicitly made the same assumption, so I should not object to this criterion. So off I went and taught the same course with different exams.

To provide a sense of what this transition was like, consider this example of the conceptual style of question. It is a traditional compare-and-contrast question on the level of ideas, and it is a question that someone in the field might entertain:

> How did Carl Rogers contrast his view of the role of values in science from the view he believed B. F. Skinner held? This difference is clear in his discussion of the five elements of an applied science of human behavior and in his two-pronged analysis that leads to a discussion of an educational example. Rogers noted a change in Skinner's views on this subject and cited an example that made the difference clear. Consider using the metaphor of evolution to describe the apparent differences between their views.

In contrast, here is how that same understanding was probed through the analysis of a specific problem that can readily be addressed using the ideas. The following is not situated in a professional debate context but aimed at how those ideas would play out in action research.

> Imagine you are asked to evaluate programs at an agency that serves homeless single people, low-income families, and non-English-speaking people.

Suppose you agree with the view held by Carl Rogers on the nature of scientific inquiry, and the agency leaders ask you to identify the *most effective* way to allocate the financial and labor resources of the agency. Please identify all the conceptual steps you would take in planning your work and include descriptions of two questions you would address that are specific to this context. One of those questions should be scientific and one not; please identify which is which, and explain why.

The first reaction I got was from students who complained I had not taught them anything about the contexts in the questions, so how could they possibly answer the questions? In all cases we had never even mentioned the contexts in class or covered them in readings, but that was an essential part of the design of the assignment. It was the heart of Hatch's question that I was trying to answer.

Most important, when the dust settled on the semester, I learned a large percentage of students who could write a good conceptual analysis of a principle or theory were unable to use that material in a problem context that was novel to them. Looking at performance on the first version of each exam, I saw that the number of students scoring in the A range dropped from 38% to 13%, and the number of students in the F range increased from 29% to 45%. Needless to say, this was a very disturbing observation for me. I had to face the fact that students had simply gotten very good at mimicking my abstract language without really understanding it. Hatch's question to me was unfortunately right on target, and I needed to rethink my course design in a big way.

The first couple of innovations I tried were based on my knowledge of basic laboratory research on learning. Although I readily transferred the lessons from research to the formal structure of my course design, there was no effect on understanding as measured by skill in using conceptual knowledge to analyze the novel problems I had created on exams. I also looked at my evaluations of conversations I had with each student in the last 2 weeks of the semester. Borrowing an idea from Randy Bass at Georgetown, I'd spent 20 minutes with each student discussing 5 key topics from my course, especially how they were related to the student's own experiences and life plans. I had been making video recordings of these interviews for several years, and I scored them using a rubric ranging from novice to very advanced on each of the topics we talked about. About a quarter of the class each year performed at the novice level across all topics.

I really needed to find a bridge between the general ideas and the particular features of the problems I created. At this point, I benefitted greatly from being part of that Carnegie cohort as those colleagues and the foundation's scholars provided plenty of feedback and good ideas on what I might do to bring about a deep understanding in my students. A Carnegie colleague provided a good idea from Grant Wiggins (2012) that later appeared in print. In this example, a shop teacher wanted to help students develop skills on welding projects, and he put five or six examples of prior students' work on a workbench, arranged in order of quality. He asked students to estimate where their work would fit into that array so they would not be surprised by the feedback he gave them. In my version, I gave a team of four or five students examples of problem-based exam questions along with three answers for each written by previous students; all were the same length but they were poor, ordinary, or excellent in quality. I asked the students to write to each other about which was the best answer for each question and why they thought so, although I never told them what I thought.

I found another good idea in conversations about metacognition, mostly in the context of having students reflect in writing on what they have learned and how it connects with any features of their own knowledge and experience. I had been skeptical about such an indirect form of instruction, but having had no luck with getting students to see the connections between conceptual understanding and analyzing specific cases, I was ready to try a suggestion that came from reasonable colleagues. In this case, I had students use a digital portfolio tool to post their thoughts on a series of prompts that asked them to reflect on the specific sections of the content of our course. The prompts did not ask them to repeat what they had learned but to think about how their viewpoint may have changed through the reading and discussion, or how they understood their own decisions and actions in terms of the topics we had covered. This small collection of reflections captured and made explicit what each individual was thinking about what they were learning and understanding, thus the term *metacognitive* writing.

After integrating these two additions into the course, the most obvious change was in performance on the problem-based examinations. Immediately the performance on those exams jumped most of the way back to the levels I had seen when I was using the conceptual exam questions. Even though the students never saw the same problem a second time—that is, the context and specifics of the questions were always novel—there was a transfer of understanding that resulted in greater success on problems I had not taught. This was one of the criteria that Wiske (1997) and her colleagues used to measure deep understanding. In the recorded conversations with students at the end of the term, there was a subtle increase in the number of students in the most advanced category, but there were no students in the novice category anymore. The entire bottom of the distribution disappeared and never returned in subsequent years. I realized that my new ways of teaching had dramatically enhanced the kind of understanding that I cared about, as measured in students' academic performance, not just in their perceptions of learning.

These results were very gratifying, and I continued to use both innovations over the next several years. The performance on exams and in the conversations remained at high levels, suggesting that the increases were not just a cohort effect or other transient variable. Because I had undertaken the project as an inquiry into some already established innovations, I did not design the work as a research experiment using my skills as an experimental psychologist. There was no longer a need to prove generality of the results, nor was I claiming to advance theories of teaching and learning in any way. I did not use statistics to decide if learning was better; the effects were quite large, and there was no risk to anyone but me if learning gains turned out to be a false alarm. I was going to teach the course again anyway, and it made sense to try to replicate the improvement with the method that I had tried out. If the results did not occur again, I learned that the success was because of something other than my course design changes. If the success was observed again, then I would continue offering the course in the revised way. The entire point of the enterprise was to help more students learn more deeply, and it seemed to be best practice to continue with innovations that consistently drove up performance.

At first I shared my experiences with only a few friends and some casual teaching circles in my department, knowing that I had no evidence to demonstrate unequivocally that I knew precisely why learning got better. Then I thought about a previous multiyear project in which colleagues read each other's teaching designs and looked closely at the resulting learning. It was an incredibly valuable experience for me, and I learned a lot from that generous interaction among my colleagues. I saw firsthand what excellent teaching could be like, including the model of people who were continuously improving their students' learning by trying out new forms of instruction. The progress was not always a linear upward path, but I was inspired by the resilience of those instructors who kept innovating and watching closely the quality of their students' understanding. My next step was to replicate those peer interactions with colleagues at the University of Nebraska. With local followed by national funding, we held an annual two-week seminar promoting teaching as a form of inquiry into learning.

The product of the seminar was a documented narrative of what each colleague had done and what was seen in the students' understanding. Many of the examples were really clever, and they resulted in nice gains in the depth of understanding demonstrated and in the larger percentage of students who were able to do very well. As this was during the early transition of intellectual work into the digital age, we made these course narratives public on

Online course portfolios include detailed context, rationale, analysis of samples of student understanding, and reflections on future work. Such course portfolios represent snapshots of the current level of ongoing inquiry into course redesign that maximizes learning. The instructors identify challenges based on close reading of students' understanding, redesign assignments and learning activities, and evaluate their innovations based on descriptions of student understanding.

a website. The format allowed us to link the narrative to many artifacts from the course, including assignments, student writing and project examples, and systems for close evaluation of the quality of understanding. Finally, the faculty reflected on what they had learned and what they expected to do the next time they taught their class. Because it was a collection of materials organized by the structure of the inquiry into learning, we described them with Bill Cerbin's (1994) term *course portfolios*.

From the earliest days of our gallery of digital course portfolios, we saw their potential as learning objects to be used in conversations among faculty members. Our annual seminars became much better as colleagues were able to read using this new genre of intellectual work before they were asked to write in it. We also found that our website was getting hundreds of visits every month, with instructors from all around the globe popping in to see what examples they might borrow and try. When this bit of work became visible through the Carnegie Foundation's continued support of collaboration on learning, we were invited by the Pew Charitable Trusts to develop a multiple-university version of the local project. For four years we had parallel operations at Indiana University, University of Michigan, Texas A&M University, and Kansas State University. Each campus had its own version of peer collaboration and mutual reading, being a very rich version of peer review of teaching and learning. Once a year we gathered the whole gang for further sharing and exchange of good practices and outstanding student understanding. The body of work that came from this collaboration was truly amazing to behold, and it was a golden time in the teaching lives of the participants.

I think the intercampus phase of the work was a very important turning point for our conversations about teaching. First, we had some validation of teaching efforts and the learning products: people from other universities were paying attention, reading the work, importing the practices and narratives, and citing the sources in conversations and conferences. Second, there was an increased exchange of insights and innovations in teaching among the university communities, and it frequently crossed disciplinary boundaries.

A teaching and learning conversation at one university was now informed by practices and successes from other universities, and those who participated in this larger community were seen locally as valuable sources of news from outside. This was taking place in the late 1990s, before the rise of many discipline-specific teaching journals and well before the wonderful presence of digital and open access journals that we enjoy now. These early pioneers in scholarship of teaching and learning (SoTL) were the cosmopolitans who brought home new ideas from their intellectual travels.

When I had the opportunity to work with colleagues in the Center for Teaching Excellence at the University of Kansas, we introduced the idea of course portfolios as the natural product of participation in funded faculty seminars and institutes. The reflection occurring in constructing a portfolio is a great benefit to each author, and the products can be shared with local colleagues and teaching scholars elsewhere as examples of systematic inquiry into teaching and learning. Reading about the experience of colleagues and the impact on their students' understanding has been both richly informative and highly motivating for instructors looking to include innovations in their teaching. These public reports serve as learning objects for instructors around the world.

Although there have been outstanding educational research journals for much longer than this narrative includes, that body of work is properly addressed to generalizable principles of learning and to the evolution of theories of education and of learning in the broadest sense. The audience for that work, like most disciplinary fields, is other scholars who are engaged in similar issues and challenges and who are deeply versed in the intellectual tools of the field. The presence of that large and impressive body of work, for better or for worse, did not made much of a dent in the practices of the professoriate in general. It appears that we may be from the same species as our students, in that many of us failed to appreciate the powerful utility of the conceptual

Brad Osborne (2017) used enhanced feedback, better scaffolding, and more explicit guides to scholarly writing to enhance students' abilities to analyze complex music. Susan Marshall (2012) transformed a psychology lecture course using contemporary hybrid formats, providing an opportunity to examine learning and look for methods that helped students understand more. Susan Stagg-Williams (2012) reversed a trend toward markedly lower performance when practice on the most difficult skills in chemical engineering was moved from homework to in-class working groups supplemented by brief instructor talk-alouds on doing the problems.

work done in educational research. That phenomenon makes some sense if we remember that deep learning often starts by using examples that are close to the learner's experience. Or perhaps, also like my students, we could mimic those ideas in conversation, but we rarely put them deep into our practices of instructional design.

I think there has been a very important place for the widespread emergence of very publicly accessible learning objects that include excellent, specific examples of inquiry into innovative design and close reading of student understanding. These learning objects may not drive theory, and the portfolio reports certainly don't qualify as educational research, but they have been incredibly powerful as change agents in the culture of higher education practice. In that sense, this intellectual work may be one of the highest forms of that elusive genre called SoTL. These practical learning objects are made very public and shared around so that colleagues can use their insights, build on and advance their practices, and offer thorough discussions and critiques of their contributions.

References

Cerbin, W. (1994). The course portfolio as a tool for continuous improvement of teaching and learning. *Journal on Excellence in College Teaching, 5*(1), 95–105.

Marshall, S. (2012). *Transforming a traditional lecture-based course to online and hybrid models of learning*. Retrieved from https://cte.ku.edu/portfolios/marshall# summary

Osborne, B. (2016). *Expanding understanding of musical forms through scholarly writing*. Retrieved from https://cte.ku.edu/chrp/portfolios/osborn

Stagg-Williams, S. (2012). *The hybrid course experience*. Retrieved from https://cte .ku.edu/portfolios/swilliams

Wiggins, G. (2012, Nov. 12). On Feedback: 13 practical examples per your requests [Web log post]. Retrieved from https://grantwiggins.wordpress.com/2012/11/04/ on-feedback-13-practical-examples-per-your-requests/

Wiske, M. S. (1997). *Teaching for understanding: Linking research with practice*. San Francisco, CA: Jossey-Bass.

16

THE SoTL CONFERENCE

Learning While Professing

Jennifer Meta Robinson

I retain a composite afterimage of the many academic conferences I have attended. In a wheel-shaped hotel lobby, several stories high, people cluster in animated conversation. Hallways like spokes lead off to more halls of upholstered rooms with pitchers of water and rows of chairs where tightly performed talks roll out in polite sequence under the flicker of advancing slides. The atmosphere, in my mind's eye, is dampened yet breathless. Occasionally, sparks of laughter or group chatter spill past the doors. I know my place in these rooms, up front or somewhere near the back. I take notes, walk the gangways, and sip small cups of lukewarm coffee. I navigate by bathrooms, registration tables, and egresses. I indulge in the suspense of snacks—will it be pretzels this time, seductive cookies, or that high bar I once encountered: ice cream sundaes?

There's a big room, usually, for the big voices, and another, sometimes a sports arena, for the texts. I frequent both, hunting for the unexpected latest, discounts on the greatest, and any gaps I might be able to perceive and even fill. If I am lucky, I'm wandering an anthropology expo, dense with books and also lively with resin skeletons, fossil mock-ups, and intriguing hand tools.

These conferences held in dedicated spaces are convenient and practical. Sometimes they are adjacent to an airport, making shuttling a fait accompli. They often feature escalated lines of scholars smoothly sliding by each other. Sometimes, dedicated walkways lead from the main hotels to the conference center, avoiding the weather, the traffic, and the neighborhood. These events are impressive, daunting, historic, progenetic. Careers as well as entire lines of intellectual thought are proposed, interviewed, reviewed, refuted, and festschrifted in these places.

I go, of course, for two main reasons: to share what I know and to learn what others have to say. Academic conferences are places of teaching and learning. They are also, like all social sites of learning, places to practice identities, relations to knowledge, and positions to others present or absent. I can read a published article, sure, but I also value being close to the people who have expertise, to follow close up the moves their minds make, to see what I can about who they are. I want to hear their voices, where they speak with certainty and when they pause. I go to fill up on ideas.

The marvel of coordination that is an academic conference is made possible by a relatively small team of worker bees as well as by the faith of a larger community that shows up to make it live. Having chaired or cochaired two international conferences, I know the nearly endless logistical detail and the massive intellectual challenge that conference organizers must undertake, often while also working a day job as professor, administrator, or teaching center professional. Their decisions about how to build the container that will hold myriad, high-stakes performances are laden not only with exigencies of budgets, room size, sports and holiday schedules, cost, transportation, accessibility, housing, administrative support, and so on but also with values about labor, time, presence, collaboration, credit, attribution, physicality, retreat and engagement, predictability, replicability, and deviation. What modes of being and knowing does the conference facilitate, and which does it mitigate or even baffle? How does it mark cohorts of people and ideas? How does it accommodate (or encourage or discourage) emergent and alternative configurations? What forums for reflection, questions, invention, and dissent does it lay?

A scholarship of teaching and learning (SoTL) conference, fully realized in its SoTLness, offers intriguing opportunities not only to disseminate scholarship and scholarly culture but also to reflect further on the practices of teaching, learning, and the field itself. Apart from the pragmatics that sometimes limit conference options (and what those are is probably open to debate), a SoTL conference invites questions about how signature pedagogy, metamessages, theories, histories, goals, and measures contribute to its overall impact as a learning and teaching venue.

These are tricky questions. Of course, many SoTL conferences look just like my generic composite and teach many of the same tacit lessons. Arguably, they should. Indeed, because SoTL is a research-based field, one might expect its conferences to echo standard academic conference conventions by featuring not only formal events structured to disseminate and review scholarly knowledge that is generative and actionable but also supporting identity markers like name tags and logo-stamped swag. Indeed, to activate such associations may well be more important for SoTL than for, say, the field of rhetoric, which traces its roots to Aristotle. As members of a new multidisciplinary field with the theoretical underpinning to mix up traditional roles, question long-standing practices, and create alliances that disrupt the organizational status quo, some SoTL practitioners find it strategic to minimize any differences, to give their work the full measure of seriousness, quality, and institutional credit it can achieve.

Still. SoTL lends itself beautifully to metaquestioning, and the answers do not have to undermine the significance of the scholarship or the scrutiny of its review process. Given that we are talking about SoTL, we might ask the following questions. What learning and teaching opportunities can an event about teaching and learning offer? What styles and assumptions, traditions and innovations, art, science, and activism can we glean from the SoTL conference venue as it is and as it could be? What would a fully realized SoTL conference look like? What goals are espoused, and which are manifest? What might we be doing differently? What assumptions about people do we make or reproduce: Who teaches, who learns, who is present, and who is not? Who is referenced, and who remains absent? Who is invited or claimed, and who actually shows up? What do we say we are doing, and what gets done? Returning to my mind's eye, here's what I imagine based on my two decades of attending SoTL conferences, symposia, colloquia, and workshops. My view is selective, personal. Not so much an afterimage this time as an ante-image, overlaying what came before with imaginings of what could still come. It's not the only worthwhile version, as I've noted, nor does it labor with many of the limitations real conferences must, as also noted. For people new to SoTL who must decide how to use their limited time and funding, it might offer some signposts for how to navigate their choices among the growing number of meeting options.

The SoTL conference I have in mind is held on a college campus. As each college campus is different—by mission, tradition, population, and location—so too will the SoTL conference take on the flavor of its surroundings. In doing so, it follows a defining assumption in the field, in addition to responding to more generalized principles, that effective teaching and learning are responsive to context, a key component of Shulman's (1986) pedagogical content knowledge. These differences, among other advantages, become mnemonics for what one did at a particular conference, from whom one learned, what lasting effects one took away. I went to one SoTL conference in a classroom building of a design that still recalled its use by an aircraft industrialist, long and thin and perched on a steep bluff above the ocean as if ready to take flight. I've been to far too many conference presentations to remember them all, but I remember the talk I gave there, the room, the people I met, the hallway conversations I had, the collaborations that we sparked there. I went to another conference where the walls were made of local limestone with visible fossils that recalled deep history waiting to be known, and students dozed in comfortable arm chairs in front of fireplaces between classes. Another featured glass classrooms walls that made the educational values of knowledge sharing and access apparent to all passersby. I went to one in a climate so mild that the student center had no doors and the classrooms opened directly outside. I went to another in an engineering school, in which the students' success in problem-solving their waste stream showed in their school café. They had designed racks to hold hundreds of reusable mugs near a handy sink for washing up. I've been to some conferences whose planners assume attendees will take the city bus or walk the city streets to get to campus. So I did, along with many others, alongside the local knowledge workers, treading their paths, making their transfers, imagining that much more vividly what it might be like to teach and learn there. As a result, I know a bit about the awkwardness of entering a classroom late when the buses are delayed or if the way to the class is uphill or has many stairs. I've sat in classrooms during conferences in which shades automatically lower or raise with the changing sunlight; at the other end of the tech spectrum, some rooms made the Internet seem like an improbability. To sit in the chairs that students sit in and look out at the lawns, city streets, or stony courtyards they see is to know something about teaching and learning in that context that is inaccessible or, at best, abstract in an off-campus conference venue.

The SoTL conference offers opportunities like these to deepen our conversations about teaching principles and learning outcomes in higher education with the field's strength in context. New surroundings—physical, disciplinary, demographic—defamiliarize what I experience as ordinary or even invisible. They invite me to see anew and reengage with the challenges that make teaching a worthwhile career pursuit. I went to one conference that had a day care center in the courtyard outside the classroom I spoke in, which made me realize that I don't know if my university has a day care, or where it would be, or whose children would be in it. I navigated a conference in a city that doesn't label its streets and others where the logic of their signs escaped me. I have been to a couple of conferences in neighborhoods so uncomfortable to me that I swore not to wander away from the hotel again, though really what I saw was simply the commerce, styles, preferences, and problems of those who lived there every day. In these cases, I gained new appreciation for how small disconnects in culture can impede learning for newcomers. It's hardly necessary to be reminded of the built-in language barriers many international students face, but I was challenged to rethink the accommodations I make for them by a Japanese cab driver who spoke no English and, moreover, had had his larynx removed, yet managed to carry on a polite and detailed conversation with me about the election of Barack Obama, using a ring of handwritten flashcards—his language on one side and mine on the other. His detailed identification of conversational formulae brilliantly bridged our linguistic limitations. What analogues of language and culture could I use to facilitate success for English-language learners or historically underrepresented students in my classes?

The SoTL conference, especially as it approaches an immersive experience, lends us an ongoing case study. Although I hesitate to make the old parallel between schools and prisons, I am inspired by Slater's (2017) article about the profound insights of U.S. prison administrators who felt themselves to be humane and progressive until they toured prisons in Norway and Germany that make quite different assumptions about discipline and rehabilitation. As with them, the stakes are high for the contributions we in SoTL can make to quality of life. As with theirs, our work occupies a civic space fraught with a complex array of social, economic, and environmental circumstances. Privy to an up-close examination of alternative modes of operation, educators also might have the chance to consider new ways "to implement our humanity" (Slater, 2017, p. 45). Short of holding a conference on a college campus (or a prison), countless possibilities exist for tapping the wisdom in other educational settings. Field trips to nearby colleges can yield many exceptional examples: a particular lecturer or lesson, a hands-on lab, a café-style classroom, innovative technology, and so on, or trips to museums, archives, cinemas, zoos, public gardens, libraries, bookstores, factories, trading floors, power stations, art studios, master classes, and theaters. Approached in a SoTL frame of mind, what alternative pedagogical methods would these places open? Which students might we better reach? How would we know? Such comparisons are the stuff of knowing about the present as we plan for the future.

Clearly, the SoTL conference I have in mind occupies a range of possibilities for gathering late-breaking news of scholarship, for defamiliarizing our assumptions about higher education, and for inspiring new modes of practice. Inevitably, it also teaches us about the values of the field itself. Consider the pedagogy expressed through the conference program's design, the way it expects to play out, the activities it facilitates on its main page and at the margins. Although many SoTL presentations rely on PowerPoint to good effect, the conference format often supports other instrumentation as well such as roundtables, poster sessions, methods workshops, writing-intensive sessions, Twitter and social media feeds (and the workshops that teach newcomers how to use them).

Some conferences offered by the International Society for the Scholarship of Teaching and Learning provide space for a teaching commons,

Founded in 2004, the International Society for the Scholarship of Teaching and Learning is the premier organization for SoTL scholars. It holds annual conferences in diverse countries, with an emphasis on North America. Its published conference pedagogy, those assumptions that have coalesced into "an approach to knowledge-sharing at the conference," emphasizes activities and dispositions that are "scholarly, engaged, inclusive, and collegial" (ISSOTL Conference Pedagogy, 2018). Its website also lists conference themes and organizers; people and events that can be considered ancestors, siblings, and offspring of SoTL and numerous events around the world, including related international conferences (www.issotl.com).

bringing into practice the concept Huber and Hutchings (2005) describe, "in which communities of educators committed to inquiry and innovation come together to exchange ideas about teaching and learning and use them to meet the challenges of educating students for personal, professional, and civic life" (p. 1). The annual SoTL Commons Conference, founded in 2007 and organized by Georgia Southern University, nominates that notion annually as crucial to the field.

As at many disciplinary conferences, official subgroupings slice the larger whole into more manageable interest groups and communities. In SoTL, they organize around such issues as research methods, teaching methods, discipline, institutional type, pedagogy, and demographics. Members may serve as collegially critical sounding boards for ideas, or they may make presentations or publish together. Membership in multiple groups helps to cross-pollinate intellectually as well as socially. In addition, conference design can invite people into the community and suggest pathways for meaningful participation in scholarly attainment and leadership roles. *The* SoTL conference, then, would incorporate diverse participation structures to facilitate diverse, circulating groups of people all invested in sharing their systematic studies as they work on complementary research agendas and a more equitable educational future.

Although I may want to absorb new ideas and jar my complacency with new situations, in truth the unfamiliar can also be a shock. At an interdisciplinary conference, the study design, evidence, conclusions, and participation that I have been enculturated by my training to expect may be quite different from what I find. If I go expecting teaching tips, I may find learning theory. If I go expecting graphed trends, I may find ethnography. If I go expecting a case study, I may find learning analytics. If I want classroom research, I may stumble into a teaching center study or a philosophy-based treatise. A good conference program will offer ways to navigate these differences. More likely, though, participants at a SoTL conference will need to attune themselves to the diversity of simultaneous discussions possible. Perhaps, as they say, such diversity is a feature not a bug.

Sometimes I approach a conference as if it were a seminar just for me. I attend sessions that help me bone up on a method or literature, what people are learning and reading right now about data analytics or graduate education or communities of practice. But one might go equally validly with the defining SoTL question: What do we gain when disciplinary experts do educational research on their own teaching and learning contexts? Put another way, what makes SoTL a viable hypothesis? I was surprised at a SoTL conference to be posed almost exactly this line of inquiry by a woman standing next to me in the buffet line. She asked if I worked at a teaching center or in administration, and when I said I was a departmental faculty member, she asked in astonishment, "What are *you* doing *here?*" What, indeed! In several days of conferencing I had heard more papers about faculty and students than by them. Searching for a riposte, I wanted one suitable not only for the buffet line but also for those who have thought conscientiously about whether learning can be measured meaningfully, have scrutinized the institutional cultures within which teaching and learning operate, or have engaged faculty and students as partners in improvement. My interlocutor made a fair question, especially in a world thick with conferences of varying value on educational research, scholarly teaching, and professional development. She wondered, it seems, where we were and who we were. How does one know one is attending a SoTL conference? What (and who) does a good SoTL conference offer that other educational conferences do not? Does that difference come through clearly in a signature SoTL conference pedagogy?

The reflexiveness of a SoTL conference is perhaps its greatest asset. It's a place where it should be possible for discourses underlying our work to surface and for us to decide when to perpetuate and when to remake them. SoTL conferences are already distinctive, tending to be collegial, international, multidisciplinary gatherings open to a fair degree of

Pain (2017) offered succinct advice from numerous scholars at various stages of their careers about how to get the most out of attending conferences. Their responses were organized by various questions: Why do you go to conferences? How do you decide which conferences to go to? Do you make a point to talk to people at coffee breaks and go to social events? What do you do after a conference is over to make sure you're maximizing the benefit?

intellectual latitude. At the same time, attendees embrace the ethical implications of teaching and the importance of its study with seriousness, passion, and inventiveness. The keynotes generally offer elucidating frameworks to guide next steps in the field as a whole. In the best instances, they serve as organizing touchstones throughout the rest of the conference, informing corridor conversations and sending session presenters scurrying with last-minute revisions. Questions tend to be constructive rather than grandstanding. Hallway moments, talking with editors, trying local cuisine with friends and colleagues, strategizing for back home are all reasons to go. Perhaps no single conference can hit all these marks, but fortunately for SoTL, reflexiveness about how goals and outcomes align is built in. As its conferences increase in number and variety, so too do our opportunities to reflect. A place there is waiting for us.

References

Huber, M. T., & Hutchings, P. (2005). *The advancement of learning: Building the teaching commons.* San Francisco, CA: Jossey-Bass.

ISSOTL Conference Pedagogy. (2018). *International Society for the Scholarship of Teaching and Learning.* Retrieved from http://www.issotl.com/issotl15/node/257

International Society for the Scholarship of Teaching and Learning. (2014). Retrieved from http://www.issotl.com

Pain, Elisabeth. (2017, May 8). How to get the most out of attending conferences. *Science.* Retrieved from http://www.sciencemag.org/careers/2017/05/how-get-most-out-attending-conferences/

Shulman, L. S. (1986). Those who understand: Knowledge growth in teaching. *Educational Researcher, 15*(2), 4–14.

Slater, D. (2017, July–August). Prison break: Can Norway style prisons work in North America? *Mother Jones.* Retrieved from https://www.motherjones.com/crime-justice/2017/07/north-dakota-norway-prisons-experiment/

CONTRIBUTORS

Carol Berenson is an educational development consultant at the University of Calgary's Taylor Institute for Teaching and Learning. An interdisciplinary background in philosophy, sociology, and women's studies informs her approach to collaboration, consultation, research, and program development in teaching and learning. Berenson's current research interests include the flipped classroom, peer observation of teaching programs, teaching controversial issues, and diversity and inclusion in teaching and learning.

Dan Bernstein was professor of psychology and director of the Center for Teaching Excellence at the University of Kansas from 2002 to 2014. Previously at the University of Nebraska–Lincoln, he taught large introductory courses, advanced undergraduate courses, and graduate seminars. Midcareer he switched from research on learning and motivation to in situ inquiry into student learning followed by a focus on electronic course portfolios centered on student learning that showcase teaching practices that yield high-quality student work. Through grants he developed team-designed assignments and scaffolding, explored using assessment data in curriculum change, and promoted interactive learning in humanities instruction. Previous grants supported a substantive peer review of the intellectual work in teaching, resulting in *Making Teaching and Learning Visible* (Bernstein, Burnett, Goodburn, & Savory; Jossey-Bass, 2006). He is a past president of the International Society for the Scholarship of Teaching and Learning and of the Society for the Experimental Analysis of Behavior.

Lendol Calder is professor of history at Augustana College in Illinois. In 1999 as a fellow at the Carnegie Academy for the Scholarship of Teaching and Learning, he began researching the problem of how to demystify historical thinking for students in gateway history courses. Calder's articles on uncoverage and the importance of metanarrative for learning have become classics of history SoTL literature. "The Stories We Tell" (*OAH Magazine of History 27*[3], [October 2013]: 5–8) has won the American Historical Association's Gilbert Prize honoring the best article of the year on teaching and learning in the field of history. In 2010 Calder was named the Illinois College professor of the year.

Bill Cerbin is professor of psychology and founding director of the Center for Advancing Teaching and Learning at the University of Wisconsin–La Crosse. He is the author of *Lesson Study: Using Classroom Inquiry to Improve Teaching and Learning in Higher Education* (Stylus Publishing, 2011), which describes a large-scale project to support the use of lesson study practices in college teaching. He was a Carnegie scholar with the Carnegie Academy for the Scholarship of Teaching and Learning, class of 1998. His niche in the scholarship of teaching and learning is in applying theory and research from the learning sciences to improve teaching and learning.

Nancy L. Chick is director of faculty development and a professor of English at Rollins College. She is coeditor of *Exploring Signature Pedagogies: Approaches to Teaching Disciplinary Habits of Mind* (Stylus Publishing, 2008) and *Exploring More Signature Pedagogies: Approaches to Teaching Disciplinary Habits of Mind* (Stylus Publishing, 2012) and author of a variety of book chapters and articles on the scholarship of teaching and learning (SoTL) as a field and on the SoTL projects she's conducted. She and Gary Poole are founding coeditors of *Teaching & Learning Inquiry*, the journal of the International Society for the Scholarship of Teaching and Learning.

Anthony Ciccone is professor emeritus of French and founding director of the Center for Instructional and Professional Development at the University of Wisconsin–Milwaukee. He has served as president of the International Society for the Scholarship of Teaching and Learning and director of the Carnegie Academy for the Scholarship of Teaching and Learning. He has made presentations nationally and internationally on SoTL inquiry, provided book chapters on doing SoTL work at the institutional level, and published his own research on student reflection based on a study of student learning in his freshman seminar on comedy. With Pat Hutchings and Mary Huber, he cowrote *The Scholarship of Teaching and Learning Reconsidered: Institutional Impact and Integration* (Jossey-Bass, 2011).

Kimberley A. Grant is a postdoctoral scholar in educational development at the Taylor Institute for Teaching and Learning at the University of Calgary. While completing a doctoral program in educational research, she had the opportunity to work with preservice teachers in on-campus courses and field experiences. A past editorial manager of *Teaching & Learning Inquiry*, she values conversations that explore the relationship between educational research and the scholarship of teaching and learning and is optimistic about the potential for these fields to enrich each other.

Margy MacMillan worked at the intersection of information literacy and SoTL for more than 15 years at Mount Royal University, conducting her own work in reading and information use and supporting colleagues through the Institute for the Scholarship of Teaching and Learning. As a professor and librarian she has developed ways of navigating the varied information landscapes of disciplinary publishing and an appreciation for scholarly communication in all forms from Twitter to encyclopedias. Now an adviser at large with Project Information Literacy, she continues to work on projects that bring librarianship and the scholarship of teaching and learning together.

Karen Manarin is professor of English at Mount Royal University in Calgary where she teaches writing and literature courses. Her research interests include reading, undergraduate research, and academic identity. She is lead author of *Critical Reading in Higher Education: Academic Goals and Social Engagement* (Indiana University Press, 2015) and has also published in teaching and learning journals.

Ryan C. Martin is a professor of psychology and chair of the psychology program at the University of Wisconsin–Green Bay. His work includes "Navigating the IRB: The Ethics of SoTL" (in *Doing the Scholarship of Teaching and Learning: Measuring Systematic Changes to Teaching and Improvements in Learning*, edited by Gurung and Wilson; Jossey-Bass, 2013), which highlights the primary ethical concerns associated with SoTL and provides a series of recommendations on avoiding unethical behavior when conducting research on teaching. He served on the institutional review board at the University of Wisconsin–Green Bay for six years including three years as chair.

Trent W. Maurer is professor of child and family development and director of the School of Human Ecology Undergraduate Research Program at Georgia Southern University. He teaches courses in family science, child development, and the university honors program. His primary research interests are in the scholarship of teaching and learning (SoTL), and he has produced multiple pieces of peer-reviewed scholarship on a variety of disciplinary and interdisciplinary SoTL topics. He was named a governor's teaching fellow in 2011 by the University of Georgia Institute of Higher Education. He has received awards for his teaching and scholarship at the departmental, college, and institutional level, as well as the 2011 University System of Georgia Regents' SoTL Award. He currently chairs the International Society for the Scholarship of Teaching and Learning's Advancing Undergraduate Research Interest Group and serves on its Advocacy and Outreach Committee in addition to serving as a reviewer or on the editorial boards of numerous disciplinary and interdisciplinary SoTL journals.

Jennifer Meta Robinson is professor of practice in anthropology and directs the campuswide graduate certificate on college pedagogy at Indiana University. She formerly directed Campus Instructional Consulting and the award-winning Scholarship of Teaching and Learning Program at Indiana and is a past president of the International Society for Scholarship of Teaching and Learning. She has won several teaching and distinguished service awards and is the author of numerous articles and book chapters on the scholarship of teaching and learning (SoTL). Her recent SoTL research investigates the potential of learning analytics for SoTL, especially for addressing grade surprise. She coedited *Teaching Environmental Literacy* (Indiana University Press, 2010), among other books, and is coeditor of the SoTL book series at Indiana University Press. She speaks and consults widely on higher education and on her disciplinary research area of contemporary food issues.

Janice Miller-Young is professor of biomedical engineering and academic director of the Centre for Teaching and Learning at the University of Alberta and has taught large and small classes in engineering and general (liberal) education. Her research interests include student and faculty learning as a result of the scholarship of teaching and learning (SoTL) inquiry; she is coeditor of *Using the Decoding the Disciplines Framework for Learning Across the Disciplines* (Jossey-Bass, 2017) and has published a variety of SoTL articles using interviews to narrow the gap between novice and expert thinking.

Jessie L. Moore is director of the Center for Engaged Learning and associate professor of English: Professional Writing & Rhetoric at Elon University. Her research and publications examine the transfer of writing knowledge and practices, multi-institutional scholarship of teaching and learning (SoTL) research and collaborative inquiry, SoTL writing residencies for faculty writers, the writing lives of university students, and high-impact pedagogies. She is coeditor of *Critical Transitions: Writing and the Question of Transfer* with Chris M. Anson (WAC Clearinghouse and University Press of Colorado, 2017) and *Understanding Writing Transfer: Implications for Transformative Student Learning in Higher Education* with Randall Bass (Stylus, 2017).

Robin Mueller is an educational development consultant and faculty member at the University of Calgary's Taylor Institute for Teaching and Learning.

She supports engagement in the scholarship of teaching and learning (SoTL), consults with campus partners to strengthen teaching and learning initiatives, and supports individual teaching development. Mueller also maintains an active research agenda in three key areas: inquiry-based learning in higher education, SoTL research methodology, and educational development assessment and evaluation.

Gary Poole is professor emeritus in the School of Population and Public Health in the faculty of medicine and senior scholar in the Centre for Health Education Scholarship at the University of British Columbia. He is a past president of the Society for Teaching and Learning in Higher Education and of the International Society for the Scholarship of Teaching and Learning and has received career achievement awards from both societies. Poole is author or coauthor of chapters in the scholarship of teaching and learning (SoTL)–related publications, and he has numerous SoTL publications in peer-reviewed journals. Poole coedits *Teaching & Learning Inquiry* with Nancy L. Chick.

James Rhem created *The National Teaching and Learning FORUM* in 1990 and has served as its executive editor from the beginning. He also created "The Teaching Professor," "Academic Leader," and a number of other newsletter publications for higher education. He is series editor of the books in the New Pedagogies and Practices for Teaching in Higher Education series from Stylus Publishing. For over 10 years he served as faculty in the "Bootcamp for Profs." He's long had a passion for teaching but is well-acquainted with research. His analysis of the teacher archetype as portrayed in American film from 1939 to the present appears as a chapter in *Teaching, Learning, and Schooling in Film: Reel Education* (Routledge, 2015). He also contributed the chapter "Ellen Langer: Philosophy, Autobiography and the Healing Quest" to *Critical Mindfulness: Exploring Langerian Models* (Springer, 2016) on the work of Harvard psychologist Ellen Langer.

David J. Voelker is associate professor of humanities and history at the University of Wisconsin–Green Bay, where he has taught since 2003. He served as codirector of the Wisconsin Teaching Fellows & Scholars program for University of Wisconsin System's Office of Professional and Instructional Development from 2013 to 2019. He has facilitated many workshops on teaching and learning, including sessions on getting started with the scholarship of teaching and learning and on using reflective dialogues in the classroom. His publications include *Big Picture Pedagogy: Finding Interdisciplinary Solutions to Common Learning Problems* (Jossey-Bass, 2017), with coeditor Regan A. R. Gurung, and "The End of the History Survey Course: The Rise and Fall of the Coverage Model," with coauthor Joel M. Sipress (*Journal of American History*, 97[4], [March 2011]: 1050–1066).

INDEX

institutions, the editors present a pioneering extension of the concept of signature pedagogy from the professions to the academic disciplines. They demonstrate how faculty members from an entire state system can collaborate as a powerful community of scholars."—*Lee S. Shulman, President, The Carnegie Foundation for the Advancement of Teaching; and Charles E. Ducommun Professor of Education Emeritus, Stanford University*

How do individual disciplines foster deep learning and get students to think like disciplinary experts? With contributions from the sciences, humanities, and the arts, this book critically explores how to best foster student learning within and across the disciplines.

Exploring More Signature Pedagogies

Approaches to Teaching Disciplinary Habits of Mind

Edited by Nancy L. Chick, Aeron Haynie, and Regan A. R. Gurung

Foreword by Anthony A. Ciccone

"No one is doing more to advance our knowledge of how the disciplines construct teaching and learning than the teacher-scholars who have collaborated on this and a predecessor volume examining disciplinary habits of head, hand, and heart in the classroom. Here are honest, fresh assessments of the state of the art of teaching across a wide variety of fields, with thoughtful attention to unsettled questions, international differences, and the changing nature of the disciplines in recent years." —*Lendol Calder, Professor of History, Augustana College*

This companion volume to *Exploring Signature Pedagogies* covers disciplines not addressed in the earlier volume and further expands the scope of inquiry by interrogating the teaching methods in interdisciplinary fields and a number of professions, critically returning to Lee S. Shulman's origins of the concept of signature pedagogies. This volume also differs from the first by including authors from across the United Stwates, as well as Ireland and Australia.

22883 Quicksilver Drive

Sterling, VA 20166-2019   Subscribe to our e-mail alerts: www.Styluspub.com

Also available from Stylus

Overcoming Student Learning Bottlenecks

Decode the Critical Thinking of Your Discipline

Joan Middendorf and Leah Shopkow

Foreword by Dan Bernstein

"Middendorf and Shopkow provide an accessible and long-needed volume that speaks to both faculty and professional developers. Drawing on their expansive experiences and research, they articulate a wide range of contexts for applying the decoding methodology to strengthen faculty's epistemological underpinnings, transform teaching and learning, and inform strategies for curricular development. This valuable resource is accessible across disciplinary, institutional, and international contexts."—*Kathy Takayama, Director, Center for Advancing Teaching and Learning Through Research, Northeastern University*

This is a book for faculty who want their students to develop disciplinary forms of reasoning and are interested in a methodology with the potential to transform and reinvigorate their teaching. It is particularly suitable for use in communities of practice and should be indispensable for any one engaged in cross-disciplinary teaching, as it enables coteachers to surface each other's tacit knowledge and disciplinary assumptions.

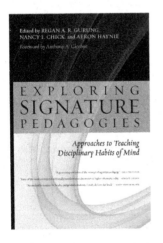

Exploring Signature Pedagogies

Approaches to Teaching Disciplinary Habits of Mind

Edited by Regan A. R. Gurung, Nancy L. Chick, and Aeron Haynie

Foreword by Anthony A. Ciccone

"This volume sets out to create conceptual and empirical bridges between the scholarship of teaching and learning and the emerging study of signature pedagogies. Drawing upon the talents of gifted scholar-teachers from across the University of Wisconsin's statewide array of fine

(Continues on preceding page)